Why You Have Not Committed
The Unforgivable Sin

Finding Forgiveness for the Worst of Sins

Page 57

Handed down
to Aline Love mom

Jeremy Myers

Redeeming Press
Publishing within the Kingdom of God

Why You Have Not Committed the Unforgivable Sin
© 2012 by Jeremy Myers

Published by Redeeming Press
Dallas, OR 97338
RedeemingPress.com

Discover other titles by Jeremy Myers at Tillhecomes.org

Get future e-books by Jeremy Myers for free by signing up for his
email newsletter at www.tillhecomes.org/subscribe/

Library of Congress Cataloging-in-Publication Data

Myers, Jeremy, 1975-
    Why you have not committed the unpardonable sin:
    Finding forgiveness for the Worst of Sins / Jeremy Myers.
    p. cm.
    ISBN: 978-0615654577 (Paper)
    ISBN: 978-1-939992-03-1 (Mobi)
    ISBN: 978-1-939992-04-8 (ePub)
    1. Sin   2. Forgiveness   3. Freedom   4. Myers, Jeremy, 1975-.   I.
Title

For Jeff, Terri, Haley, Andrew, Nadia, Jamie,
and the scores of others who have contacted
me over the years about the unpardonable sin.

I hope the love and forgiveness of God overwhelms you.

Table of Contents

YOU HAVE NOT COMMITTED THE UNFORGIVABLE SIN

Be encouraged. You have not committed the unforgivable sin. You are not eternally damned. You are not forsaken by God. You are not hated by God. You are not outside the bounds of His love and grace.

Quite to the contrary, you are loved by God more than you possibly know. You are forgiven. You are accepted. Eternal life is still yours. God wants you in His family, enjoying all the blessings and privileges of the Kingdom of God.

You might be skeptical. You might doubt these words. You might be afraid. You might have done or said some very bad things, or thought something evil, and are scared that God has cut you off forever. But stick with me through this book, and by the end, you will see that there is nothing which can separate you from the love, acceptance, and forgiveness of God.

You can have peace. You can have joy. You can know without a doubt that God loves you.

You may be thinking, "But you don't know what I've done! You don't know what I've said! You don't know what I've thought!"

That is true; I don't. But it does not matter. From what I know about God, what I know from Scripture, and what I know about sin and the Gospel, I can say with absolute confidence that you have not committed the unforgivable sin.

JAMIE'S STORY

Jamie was in her early twenties and was attending a college in North Carolina when she contacted me online. She sent to me an email full of fear and concern for her eternal destiny. She was terrified that she had committed the unforgivable sin. A year earlier her pastor preached a sermon called "The Unpardonable Sin" based on Matthew 12:31-32. The text says this:

> Therefore I say to you, every sin and blasphemy will be forgiven men, but the blasphemy against the Spirit will not be forgiven men. Anyone who speaks a word against the Son of Man, it will be forgiven him; but whoever speaks against the Holy Spirit, it will not be forgiven him, either in this age or in the age to come.

The pastor preached that the unpardonable sin, the sin that would not be forgiven, was the sin of blasphemy against the Holy Spirit. This sin, he said, is when you tell the Holy Spirit you hate Him; when you tell Him to leave you alone; when you say bad words at the Holy Spirit. When you do this, the pastor said, the Holy Spirit will leave you forever, and God will never forgive you for saying such words, and you will be condemned to hell for all eternity.

Jamie wrote in her email that it frightened her to learn about a sin that could cut her off forever from God, and worse yet, she could not stop thinking about this sin. She said that the words, "I hate you, Holy Spirit" tumbled around in her mind for hours on end. She wrote in her email that she silently said the words in her mind over and over and over, terrified that they were going to pass her lips, and she would be eternally condemned. Often she feared that thinking the words was the same as saying them. The words haunted her at night. They entered her nightmares, and she was scared she might say the words while she slept.

Later that week, her boyfriend broke up with her, she got in a car accident, and she flunked a chemistry exam, all on one day. She was so angry that she went home, locked herself in her room, and shouted out, "F*** you, Holy Spirit! I hate you!"

And with that, she knew she was eternally condemned, consigned to burn in the pit of hell forever. She was certain God hated her now, that God would never forgive her for saying such things.

Despair set in. She figured her life didn't matter anymore. Why go on living if all she had to look forward to was eternal punishment in hell? She started contemplating suicide. She experimented with drugs to numb the pain. She slept around with any guy who would have her. Also, since she had already spoken the blasphemy against the Holy Spirit, these words became her daily mantra. Instead of reading her Bible and praying as she used to do, she cursed the Holy Spirit every chance she got.

All of these behaviors convinced her more and more that she had committed the unforgivable sin. After all, a true Christian would not do and say such things. These things were evidence that God had truly abandoned her and given her over to Satan to be taught not to blaspheme and to suffer eternally for what she said. Suicide began to seem more and more appealing.

And yet deep down inside, a glimmer of hope remained. Somewhere during her slide into sin, she spent some time researching online about the unforgivable sin, and she found a website which said that suicide was the unforgivable sin because it was the only sin which you could not repent of afterwards. A person could repent of all other sins and receive forgiveness, but not suicide because once your life was over there was no opportunity for repentance.

This thought kept her from taking her own life. What if her pastor had been wrong and she had not committed the unpardonable sin after all? What if this website was correct and it was suicide that was the unforgivable sin? If that was so, then as long as she didn't commit suicide, maybe she was okay and God would still forgive her for what she had said.

So she started to reform her life. She stopped taking drugs and sleeping around. She stopped cursing the Holy Spirit, and began to read her Bible and pray again.

But every day the doubts came back. Matthew 12:31-32 said nothing about suicide. It talks about speaking against the Holy Spirit, and that is what she had done. How could she know whether or not God could forgive her? How could she know whether or not He loved her? How could she know whether or not she had committed the unforgivable sin?

It was at this time that she emailed me. I had written some articles online about the unforgivable sin as well, and she happened to find them and sent an email asking for help. Over the course of the next several months we exchanged dozens of emails as she began to learn about God's limitless grace, mercy, and love, and especially the truth of what the unpardonable sin is, and why she had not committed it. She gained new hope for her future, a new love for God, and she found a new church fellowship which relies not on fear and guilt to control its members, but teaches the complete love and forgiveness of God to give people freedom and joy in following Jesus.

MANY FEAR THEY HAVE
COMMITTED THE UNFORGIVABLE SIN

Tragically, Jamie is not alone in her experience. The pages on my website about the unpardonable sin are some of the most popular. They are nearly always in the daily top ten posts. Some of those who read these posts send me emails with questions and stories almost identical to those of Jamie. I receive numerous such emails every month.

They heard a sermon, read a book, stumbled upon a website, or attended a Bible study where they were told about the unpardonable sin and what would happen to them if they committed it, and they have lived in fear ever since. Not all fear what Jamie feared, because different people have been told different things about the unforgivable sin. Some have been told that the unforgivable sin is divorce, adultery, or abortion, and since they have done these things, they despair of ever being loved or forgiven by God.

Others have been told that the unforgivable sin is suicide, and they have a family member who committed suicide, or are contemplating suicide themselves, and fear that such a sin will result in eternal damnation.

But whatever people have been taught about the unforgivable sin, much of this teaching causes countless people to live in a constant state of fear, despair, and terror about their eternal destiny.

The real tragedy, however, is that this fear about the unpardonable sin is unwarranted and unnecessary.

Thankfully, some people who are caught in the bondage of despair about their eternal life go seeking answers. Like Jamie, they wonder if what they were told was wrong. They have a small glimmer of hope that maybe God still loves them. They think that possibly the Scriptures teach something different about the grace, love, and forgiveness of God than what they heard from their pastor or read in a book.

That is why I have written this book. Drawing from my experience in pastoral counseling and in answering the fears and questions of people who contact me through my website, this book is devoted to explaining what the unpardonable sin is and how you can know for certain that you have not committed it. Hopefully, be reading this book, you will gain freedom from the fear that you have committed the unpardonable sin, and will come to see how much God loves you.

PREVIEW OF THIS BOOK

Through this book, I want to impress upon you the good news that no matter what, there is grace for you. There is love. There is forgiveness. Even though you may have committed a terrible sin, God has already forgiven you for it. This book will show you how you can know the truth of the Scriptures about God's infinite love and eternal forgiveness for you—no matter what.

While eternal separation from God is a real possibility for many people, it is not God's will that people who love Him and want to spend eternity with Him might fear hell because of something they said or did. Such a view of God is not Scriptural. People need not fear they have committed the unforgivable sin.

Yet people are still afraid, which is why I wrote this book. Here is a summary of the following chapters: Chapter 2 will address the most common views about the unforgivable sin which are *not* based on Matthew 12:32, and will show why all of them misrepresent Scripture and what God accomplished for you through Jesus Christ. Chapter 3 will take a detailed look at Matthew 12:31-32, which is the most popular passage used to preach and teach about the unforgivable sin. Chapter 4 will then survey several of the common theories about the unpardonable sin which *are* based on the text of Matthew 12:31-32. Chapter 5 will conclude with how you can know you have not committed the unforgivable sin, and why God's love for you is infinite and His forgiveness is total and complete.

Don't live in fear any longer. Live in the freedom of forgiveness that is in Jesus Christ.

COMMON VIEWS ABOUT THE UNFORGIVABLE SIN

Most Christians have wondered at one time or another if they have committed the unpardonable sin. I remember being terrified as a child that I had committed some unknown sin which would separate me eternally from God, and so several times a day, I would ask God to forgive me of all known and unknown sins, and would once again ask God to save me and give me eternal life.

What bad things had I possibly done as a youth? Sure, I fought with my siblings, stole candy from the supermarket, and disobeyed my parents. But there were a few particular sins which terrified me most. They were terrible, and I hesitate even to write them here, as I have never told anyone about them before. But to show you that I too have struggled with the unforgivable sin, let me share one of my more terrible sins.

As a teenager, I remember kneeling at my bed late one night, and praying to Satan that he would come into my heart. This is a terrible thing to pray for, but let me explain my rationale. I had been told as a child that one became a Christian by asking Jesus into their heart, which I had done. In fact, as I indicated in the previous paragraph, I had done this numerous times. But one day, someone told me that God was stronger than Satan, and once Jesus was in your heart, nothing could remove Him; not even Satan.

So I decided to test it. I prayed to Satan that he would enter my heart. I also prayed that if he was successful, he would make me the antichrist. I figured that if I was going to go down in flames, I might as well make it count.

I remember waiting for something to feel different, but nothing seemed to change, and so I decided that Jesus must have been successful in keeping Satan out of my heart.

But nevertheless, for many years afterwards, I had an unshakable fear that maybe Satan had been successful, and since he was the great deceiver, I would not know that he ruled my heart until I actually became the antichrist. And so I began to pray night and day that God would keep me from becoming the antichrist. One of my greatest fears at that time was that I would grow up to be God's greatest enemy on earth.

You can imagine that among the theories on what the unpardonable sin is, one of the top contenders is asking Satan to kick Jesus out of your heart and take up residence there himself so that you can become the antichrist. If anyone has committed the unpardonable sin, it is me.

If I had gone for counseling from a pastor who warns others about the unforgivable sin, I believe he would have told me I was doomed forever; that there was no forgiveness for me. I also believe that if such a pastor reads this book, the incident I have just shared will convince them that I did indeed commit the unpardonable sin, and therefore, they will say that this book contains the heresy of a reprobate whose heart has been darkened by Satan's lies.

But I hope that you will read the book and determine for yourself—in the light of Scripture and through the guidance of the Holy Spirit—if what these pages contain is true. The content of this book contains some of the things I have learned over the years about the unforgivable sin, and how I gained freedom and deliverance from my sins of the past, coming to an understanding of God's infinite love, grace, and forgiveness for someone like me.

This chapter addresses the most common views on what the unpardonable sin is and will briefly show that while these behaviors are sinful, they are not the unforgivable sin. Instead, Scripture shows that these sins are clearly forgivable by God.

TWO TYPES OF UNFORGIVABLE SINS

There are two types of sins that people often consider "unforgivable." The first type is based on Matthew 12:31-32 where Jesus says that blasphemy against the Holy Spirit is a sin that will not be forgiven. It is taught that though the people who commit this sort of sin often wish to repent afterwards, this sin is so grievous to God He will never forgive it. It is taught that once a person commits this sin, God will utterly reject and deny such a person, no matter how much they repent or plead for forgiveness. This is properly referred to as "the unforgivable (or unpardonable) sin" and will be the focus of chapters 3–5.

The rest of this chapter focuses on the second type of unforgivable sin. This second type is considered to be unforgivable because the nature of the sin does not allow the person to properly repent. Many Christians throughout the world believe that if you sin, you must repent of that sin and ask God for forgiveness. If you do not repent, or if you die without repenting, then you will not be forgiven for that sin, and hence, it is unforgiven.

These sins are not based on the text of Matthew 12:31-32, but are still considered unforgivable because it is believed that a person cannot properly repent of such sins.

Although such sins are not technically "the unforgivable sin," I will deal with them in this chapter since so many people live in a constant state of fear and guilt after committing one of these sins. These sins most commonly include divorce, adultery, abortion, and suicide.

IS DIVORCE UNFORGIVABLE?

Some believe that divorce is unforgivable. This view is not as common as it once was. After all, roughly fifty percent of Christians are divorced. Common sins such as divorce usually make poor candidates for the unforgivable sin since such a position would disqualify most Christians from eternal life. However, there are still some who believe that divorce is unforgivable.

The logic of this view is primarily based upon Malachi 2:16, where God says, "I hate divorce." Those who quote this verse usually overlook the fact that Scripture lists other sins which God also hates, such as pride, lying, and discord (Prov 6:16-19). Nevertheless, divorce is singled out as particularly bad, because it is thought to be a sin that people cannot properly repent of, for if someone gets divorced and then repents of it, they are still divorced. The sin still remains. For this reason, people think that divorce is unpardonable because it can never properly be repented of.

There is much to be said against this view. First, as with most views about the unpardonable sin, those who hold this view reveal a deep misunderstanding about the grace of God and what was accomplished by Jesus on the cross for the sins of the whole world. An improper understanding of the grace and forgiveness of God is the root cause of most of the wrong views about the unforgivable sin. The topics of God's infinite grace and forgiveness will be looked at later in this book, and so nothing more will be said about it here except to say that God's grace covers even divorce.

The idea that divorce is unforgivable is also disproven by various Scriptures. For example, it is critical to recognize that God Himself is a divorced person. In Jeremiah 3:8, God gives Israel a certificate of divorce. In other words, God divorced Israel. One could argue that God was not exactly married to Israel the same way that a man is married to a woman, but against this it could also be argued that the covenant relationship God has with Israel is far stronger and far more binding than the relationship shared between a husband and wife.

Some might also say that it was okay for God to divorce Israel because of her numerous acts of infidelity to Him, and infidelity is the one basis by which divorce is allowed (cf. Matt 19:9). Of course, Jesus says that the only reason for this allowance was because of the hardness of people's hearts (Matt 19:8). Ideally, not even marital infidelity should result in divorce, as in God's eyes, the marriage union lasts as long as both people live. This is even more true of God, whose patience and long-suffering are nearly without limits. Yet the limit was reached, and God gave Israel a certificate of divorce. God is a divorced person.

It is also quite likely that Moses was divorced. When God called Moses in the wilderness to go to Egypt and deliver the people of Israel from slavery, Moses' wife Zipporah begins the journey with him (Exod 4:20). But when God almost strikes Moses dead for failing to circumcise his sons, Zipporah performs the procedure. At this time, most Middle Eastern people thought that circumcision was a disgusting and reprehensible mutilation of the body, and apparently, Zipporah felt the same way. It is likely that Moses never circumcised his sons because of marital disagreement over the issue. Now, when God forces Zipporah to circumcise her sons, she is so enraged by the procedure, Moses sends her away and she takes their sons with her (Exod 18:2).

In Exodus 18, after the Israelites have escaped from Egypt and are camped at Mount Sinai, Moses' father-in-law, Jethro, tries unsuccessfully to reunite Moses and Zipporah (Exod 18:6). Though the text does not say that Zipporah went with Jethro when he returned home (18:27), we never read about Zipporah in the rest of the books of Moses. We do read about the sons of Moses (Exod 32:10; cf. 1 Chr 23:14-17), but Zipporah herself is never mentioned again. This leads many scholars to believe that Moses and Zipporah permanently separated from each other. The only reason she came back with her father Jethro in Exodus 18 is to give Moses custody of their sons.

So it is interesting to read in Matthew 19 that Moses permitted divorce. He had no choice, for he himself was divorced! Yet we know that Moses was forgiven of his separation from his wife, and will spend eternity with God and all the saints in heaven. Not only is Moses given a place of honor as a hero of faith (Heb 11:23-29), but at the Mount of Transfiguration both Moses and Elijah appear and talk with Jesus (Matt 17:3-4). Clearly, Moses did not commit an unpardonable sin in separating from his wife, Zipporah.

Divorce is forgivable, and indeed, as will be shown in chapter 5, is already completely forgiven by God just like every other sin. If you have been divorced, you need not worry about whether God loves you and has forgiven you. He loves you more than you know, and has already forgiven you in Jesus Christ. Divorce is not the unforgivable sin.

IS ADULTERY UNFORGIVABLE?

Related to the view that divorce is the unpardonable sin, some people believe that adultery is unpardonable. But most who hold this view have a special type of adultery in mind. They believe that adultery itself is forgivable. They believe that if a person sleeps with someone who is not their spouse, but then confess and repent of this sin, they can be forgiven.

However, some argue that there is a special type of adultery which can never be forgiven. This is the type of adultery that is the result of divorce and remarriage. People who hold this view believe that although God makes allowance for people to get divorced, such people may not get remarried as long as their ex-spouse lives. Why not? Because marriage lasts as long as both the husband and wife live, and if someone gets remarried after a divorce, that person is essentially living in a state of constant adultery.

This logic is drawn from Matthew 19:9 where Jesus says that anyone who is divorced and marries another commits adultery. Once again, the idea that adultery is unforgivable is based on the concept that in order for a person to go to heaven when they die, they must not have any unconfessed sin in their life. Though a person who has been divorced and remarried may be sorry for what they have done, they cannot ever fully repent of this sin because they are living in a constant state of adultery. In this way, divorce *and remarriage* becomes the unforgivable sin because the one who does this is in a constant state of sin.

As with the view that divorce itself is unforgivable, this view also is based on a faulty understanding of God's grace and the infinite forgiveness that is in Jesus Christ, which will be looked at in more detail in chapter 5.

Aside from the theological truth of the infinite forgiveness of God, numerous Scripture passages clearly refute the idea that adultery is unforgivable. First, pretty much all of the forefathers of Israel had numerous wives. While many try to explain this behavior as a practice that was normal at that time, we cannot explain away the fact of God's original plan for marriage was that it should be between one man and one woman (Gen 1:24). Therefore, even though the culture might have allowed a man to have more than one wife, the instructions of God did not. So when Abraham, Isaac, and Jacob took more than one wife for themselves, they were committing adultery. The same thing can be said for nearly all the kings of Israel, who were specifically commanded to not take multiple wives for themselves (Deut 17:16-17). Yet even King David, a man after God's own heart, had multiple wives (2 Sam 11:4; 1 Chr 3:1-9).

When we get into the New Testament where the prohibition against adultery is more clearly and frequently stated, there are numerous examples of Christians who commit adultery and yet are still considered eternal children of God. One example is in 1 Corinthians 5:1-8 where a man sleeps with his father's wife, and yet Paul clearly identifies him as a brother in Christ who has been led into serious sin (1 Cor 5:11). When confronting the rampant sexual immorality that was present in the Corinthian church, Paul does not threaten them with hell and everlasting destruction, but with the theological truth that as believers in Christ who have been raised with Him, we should not behave in such a manner (1 Cor 6:12-20).

Scripture is clear that while adultery is a sin, it is forgivable, even for people like Abraham, Isaac, Jacob, and David who lived in a lifelong state of adultery. Adultery is not the unforgivable sin.

IS ABORTION UNFORGIVABLE?

Some people believe that abortion is the unforgivable sin. However, there is no biblical or theological support for this idea. Some might argue that killing a baby is one of the worst types of murder since babies are innocent, but if this were so, why would infanticide not be unforgivable? Do children become less innocent the moment they depart the mother's womb? No, I suspect that most who teach that abortion is unforgivable are simply trying to scare women into not having an abortion.

What many fail to realize is that women who undergo abortions often have terrible choices to face in life, and typically have been abandoned by the man who impregnated them. Fearful that they may not be able to take care of themselves and a baby, some women choose to terminate their pregnancy. They are faced with a difficult decision, and must not be judged or condemned too harshly.

At the same time, however, it must be noted that abortion truly does take the life of another person. It is not like shooting someone with a gun, but it is nevertheless a form of murder. But note this, if abortion is unforgivable, then all forms of murder are unforgivable, and this view is completely indefensible when compared with Scripture.

Numerous people in the Bible committed murder and were forgiven by God and accepted into His family. Moses murdered an Egyptian (Exod 2:12), David had Uriah killed (2 Sam 11:14-17), and even Paul went about arresting and killing Christians before he became one of the greatest missionaries the world has ever seen (Acts 8:1-3). Even when it comes to killing children, many Israelite people fell into the sin of sacrificing their children to false idols (Ezek 16:21).

Nevertheless, such sin did not keep God from promising to remember His covenant with the people of Israel and provide atonement for them (Ezek 16:60-63). If God can forgive people like Moses, David, Paul, and the idol-worshipping Israelites, God will also forgive every mother who has had an abortion. Abortion is not the unforgivable sin. There is complete grace and forgiveness for women who have abortions.

IS SUICIDE UNFORGIVABLE?

Finally, there is the teaching that suicide is unforgivable. When it comes to sinful actions that are unforgivable, this is the most common view. Once again, as with the other sinful actions, the reason people feel that suicide is unforgivable is because there is no opportunity to repent from this sin after a person commits it. Many people wrongly believe that if you die with unrepented and unconfessed sin in your life, God will not let you into heaven. When someone commits suicide their last living action was the sin of self-murder, and since they are unable to repent of this sin afterwards, some people feel that suicide will keep a person out of heaven.

Tragically, due to this idea, many surviving families of suicide victims not only have to deal with the terrible loss of losing a loved one in such a horrible way, but also have to deal with the pain, fear, and incredible sorrow of thinking that their loved one is now in hell, even though they may have been a wonderful Christian for most of their life. The pain of losing a family member to suicide is hard enough. The pain of losing a family member *eternally* to the fires of hell because of suicide is too much to bear for most families, and it destroys the rest of their lives.

This should not be, especially since it is not true. Suicide is forgivable. How do we know this? First of all, as with every sinful action we can possibly commit—including suicide—Scripture is clear that God forgives all such sins. I will explain in detail how we can know this in chapter 5, and will also explain why confession and repentance are not required to receive divine forgiveness of sins.

But specifically regarding the sin of suicide, Scripture records several examples of men who committed suicide, but who will be in heaven with God for eternity. For example, Samson committed suicide (Judg 16:29-30) but Hebrews 11:32 lists Samson as a great example of a man of faith. Would God include someone in a list of people of great faith who actually ended up in hell? Of course not. What kind of example would that be?

An even clearer example however, is King Saul. He also committed suicide and even led his armor bearer to do the same (1 Sam 31:4-5; 1 Chr 10:4-5). Yet when King David rises to the throne, he composes a song in honor of King Saul (2 Sam 1:19-27). In the middle of this song, David, under the inspiration of God, says that King Saul and his son, Jonathan, are not divided in death (2 Sam 1:23). Nobody questions that Jonathan is with God in heaven, and if he will spend eternity with God, then so will King Saul.

Though some people think David just means that Saul and Jonathan were buried together, David knows how to talk about burying people in a grave (Psa 5:9; 6:5; 30:3; 31:17; 141:7), and says nothing of the sort here. If David only meant that Saul and Jonathan were buried together, he would have said so and would have included Saul's other sons, Abinidab and Malchishua, in his statement, since they also were buried together with Saul and Jonathan (cf. 1 Sam 31:2 with 1 Chr 10:12). No, under divine inspiration, David recognizes that Saul and Jonathan were reunited after death for eternity with God. Suicide did not keep Saul out of heaven, nor will it keep any other person out of heaven. Suicide is not the unforgivable sin.

In the past when I have taught this in various churches and conferences, I have been warned afterwards that I should not teach such things, even if it is true, because it will encourage people to commit suicide. Apparently, some fear that if we teach that people can go to heaven even if they commit suicide, those who are thinking about suicide will be more likely to go through with it. It is better, they say, to teach that suicide is unforgivable because this idea will hopefully keep people from committing suicide.

I strongly disagree. We do not encourage people to do what is right by lying to them. We cannot scare people into obedience. People are encouraged to do the right thing by telling them what is true and right. The truth, if properly taught, encourages right living and behavior. The same goes for the truth that suicide is forgivable.

When a person is contemplating suicide, there are numerous things going on in their minds and lives which lead them to think that taking their life is the best solution to their problems. They may be dealing with deep depression, or feeling that nobody loves them, or that their best years in life are behind them and every day is worse than the one before and it would be better to just end it all right now before things get even worse. I have dealt with suicidal depression in the past, and these are some of the things I thought and felt.[1]

One thing that helps people overcome suicidal depression and anxiety is the knowledge that they are loved, needed, and wanted. They need to know that there is hope for their future, that life will get better and is worth living. While there are numerous possible sources for such love and hope, the greatest source of all is God. He loves us more than we can possibly know or imagine, and He has plans for our life and our future that are far beyond anything we can ask or imagine. He has a grand purpose for

---

[1] I have written about my experiences with depression in Alise Wright, ed., *Not Alone: Stories of Living with Depression* (Folsom, CA: Civitas, 2011).

each one of us in life, which never includes ending our life through suicide. He has a goal and purpose for our lives on earth, and if we commit suicide, we will miss out on fulfilling His perfect plan for us. This is the truth presented in Scripture, and this is the view of God which will help people work through their depression and anxiety about life without giving in to suicide.

But when we tell people that God will not forgive them if they commit suicide, we are giving them a terribly dangerous and destructive picture of God. We are telling them that God only loves them and forgives them as long as they do not sin. But as soon as they do sin, they must go begging to God for forgiveness, and if they do not, He will send them to hell for eternity. Such a God is petulant, like a spoiled child who wants everything to go his way all the time, or he won't play. This is a power-hungry God, who wants to keep people squirming under His ever-watchful eye as He waits for them to mess up so He can pounce on sinners and condemn them to everlasting hell. This view of God confirms to people their dark suspicion: God hates them.

When people are dealing with deep depression, the anxieties of life, ruined relationships, lost jobs, the death of a child or spouse, or ongoing health problems, the last thing they need is the idea that God hates them. How much better it is to know that even though they are going through some of the worst things that can be experienced in life, God still loves them, and is still with them, and will continue to be by their side for the rest of their life and for eternity—no matter what? This view of God does not encourage people to commit suicide, but rather encourages people to have hope for the future and to believe that there is a purpose in life for them.

So teach people that suicide is forgivable, not just because this is true, but because this tells others what kind of God we serve. He is a loving and compassionate God, full of understanding in our times of weakness. He is tender with us in times of pain, and present with us when we feel abandoned. The knowledge of this truth will not encourage people to commit suicide, but will help keep them from it.

Will some people still commit suicide? Tragically, yes. But not because of the idea that God is loving and forgiving, but simply because sometimes, people commit terrible sin. And if a person does commit suicide, the knowledge that God still loves and forgives that person will also be a source of great encouragement to the loved ones and family members who are left behind. They will know that although their loved one went through some terrible experiences in life, they are now free from pain and suffering and they will all be reunited again with God in eternity.

CAN GOD FORGIVE ME?

So none of the sinful actions that are sometimes considered "unforgivable" are actually unforgivable. God has forgiven all of these sins through Jesus Christ, and if you have committed any of these, He has already forgiven you too.

If there is a different sin which you believe God cannot forgive, just remember that there are a whole host of other sins mentioned in the Bible that true believers have committed, and yet they will still be in heaven. The Bible talks about believers who commit idolatry (1 Kings 11:1-10). Others believe only for a while and then fall away (Luke 8:13). We read of some who do not continue in the Word of Christ (John 8:31), do not abide in Christ (John 15:1-8), become disqualified in the race of the Christian life (1 Cor 9:24-27), or resist God's correction up to the point of physical death (1 Cor 11:30-32).

Still others stray from the faith (1 Tim 1:5-6), ship-wreck their faith (1 Tim 1:18-20), fall away from the faith (1 Tim 4:1-3), deny the faith (1 Tim 5:8), cast off initial faith to follow Satan (1 Tim 5:12-15), stray from the faith by loving money (1 Tim 6:9-10), teach false doctrine (1 Tim 6:20-21), and deny Christ and live faithless lives (2 Tim 2:11-13).

We have the examples of people in the Bible who murdered and yet are part of God's family (Jacob's sons). Other men like Solomon, Amaziah and Uzziah will most likely be in heaven, but did not live faithfully to God during their lives. There is Lot who committed incest with his daughters, Ananias and Sapphira who lied to the church and to the Holy Spirit and who died as a result, but will still be in heaven. Scripture is full of examples of people who committed almost every sort of sin, and yet by every indication, were still forgiven by God and will spend eternity with God in heaven.

The grace of God runs deeper and wider than most of us will ever know. The ocean of God's grace never runs dry. The limits of God's grace are never reached. No matter what you have done, there is forgiveness for all your sins through the grace and mercy of God.

But what about "blasphemy against the Holy Spirit"? While most believe that God can forgive us of everything we do, many also believe that there is a certain sin talked about in Matthew 12:31-32 which will never be forgiven. But as with all Scripture, the context is vital for understanding what this passage means. Chapter 3 will look at this key text.

A DETAILED LOOK AT
MATTHEW 12:31-32

The most famous passage about the unforgivable sin is
Matthew 12:31-32 (and the parallel passage in Mark 3:28-
30). Though other texts are sometimes used in connection
with this passage (e.g., Heb 6:4-6; 10:26-27; 2 Tim 2:12;
1 John 5:16), Matthew 12:31-32 is most frequently mentioned because it is the only passage which specifically
mentions a sin that will not ever be forgiven, a sin which
is called "blasphemy against the Spirit."

Since this Scripture is so crucial to the question of the
unpardonable sin, it is critical to understand what the text
means. Only then can we understand what the unpardonable sin is, and how we can know whether or not we have
committed this sin.

THE CONTEXT OF MATTHEW 12:31-32

In Matthew 12, Jesus is in the middle of a controversy
with the Jewish religious leaders of His day. He has been
performing miracles, fulfilling prophecies, and performing many signs which should have proven to the religious

leaders that Jesus was indeed the promised Messiah, just as He claimed.

In one incident, Jesus casts a demon out of a man, and although the crowd sees this as proof that Jesus was the promised Messiah, the religious leaders claim that Jesus casts out demons by the power of Beelzebub, the prince of demons (Matt 12:22-24).

As a result of this exchange with the religious leaders, Jesus says this:

> Therefore I say to you, every sin and blasphemy will be forgiven men, but the blasphemy *against* the Spirit will not be forgiven men. Anyone who speaks a word against the Son of Man, it will be forgiven him; but whoever speaks against the Holy Spirit, it will not be forgiven him, either in this age or in the *age* to come.

What did Jesus mean by this? What is this sin of blasphemy against the Spirit which will not be forgiven? There are two keys to help us understand what Jesus meant. First, we must understand the historical and cultural context in which Jesus lived, and which gave rise to this controversy between Him and the other Jewish religious leaders of His day. If we understand the historical and cultural context of Matthew 12:31-32, the true meaning of this passage begins to emerge.

Second, we must look at the Scriptural context of this passage. These verses cannot be understood in isolation from the chapters on either side of Matthew 12, and the book of Matthew as a whole. Matthew wrote his Gospel with a particular point of view in mind and a particular message to get across to a particular audience. When we understand the context, the meaning and significance of Matthew 12:31-32 becomes even clearer.

HISTORICAL-CULTURAL CONTEXT

It is critical to understand the role of "signs" in Jewish thinking and theology. In numerous passages throughout the Hebrew Scriptures, God tells the Israelites how to recognize when a person is speaking for God. God tells the Israelites to ask for a sign from the person who claims to speak in the name of God (cf. Deut 13:1-5; 18:20-22). Whenever someone came preaching and teaching in the name of God, the Hebrew people were to ask them for a miraculous or prophetic sign, which would verify or disprove this prophet's claim to be the spokesman of God.[1] So in Jewish culture, signs were looked upon as an indication that God was at work in a person's life, or as proof that the prophet's words were true (cf. Matt 11:38-39; Mark 8:11; Luke 11:16; John 6:30).

When Jesus began to teach and minister to others, much of what He was saying and doing was extremely challenging to the traditional ideas and practices of first century Judaism. So it is no surprise that Jesus performs numerous signs, wonders, and miracles *to prove* that He was who He said He was, and that He truly was proclaiming the message of God. This idea is clearly seen in the surrounding textual context of Matthew 12:31-32.

THE SCRIPTURAL CONTEXT

The book of Matthew was written primarily to a Jewish audience, and was intended to prove to them that Jesus

---

[1] Many Christians still attempt to operate under this framework, failing to recognize the church does not need signs and wonders to verify the truth. We have been given different (and better) ways of discerning the truthfulness of what pastors and teachers are saying, such as the indwelling Holy Spirit (John 16:13), and the Word of God (Acts 17:11).

was the promised Jewish Messiah. Matthew goes to great lengths to prove that Jesus had a Messianic lineage (Matt 1:1-7), fulfilled Messianic prophecy (Matt 2:5-6, 17-18, 23; etc.), received the affirmation of God (Matt 3:13-17), and performed all the Messianic expectations (Matt 11:2-19).

Matthew writes about the numerous signs which Jesus performed to prove that He was the Messiah. He healed leprosy, which only genuine prophets in Israelite history had been able to heal (Matt 8:1-4). He controlled the weather (Matt 8:23-27), cast out demons (Matt 8:28-34), heals paralysis (Matt 9:1-8), welcomes and forgives the outcasts (Matt 9:1-13), raises the dead to life (Matt 9:18-26), restores sight to the blind (Matt 9:27-31), and returns speech to the mute (Matt 9:32-34). The entire Gospel of Matthew seems to be a parade of miracles and teachings from Jesus which are intended to prove to the Hebrew people that Jesus was the promised Messiah.

All of these miracles just listed lead up to Matthew 12:31-32. In this text, Jesus criticizes the Jewish religious leaders. Despite everything He has done, they still do not believe, and in fact, say that the miracles of Jesus are performed by the power of the devil. God has made clear through Moses and the other prophets in the Hebrew Scriptures that no one who does the kinds of works Jesus was doing could be anything but a prophet of God. So Jesus warns them about their willful denial of the clear signs they have seen.

Ironically, immediately after this warning from Jesus, the religious leaders ask Jesus for another sign. They say, "Teacher, we want to see a sign from you (Matt 12:38)." This proves the point once again that in Jewish thinking, a prophet was verified by the signs that accompanied their teachings. In asking Jesus for a sign, the religious leaders prove that they are good Jewish theologians. The problem, however, is that Jesus has already given them dozens of signs. What more do they want if they will not believe the signs they have already seen?

Nevertheless, Jesus promises to give them something more and greater. He promises to give them "the sign of Jonah." As Jonah was three days in the belly of a fish, so also Jesus will be three days and three nights in the heart of the earth (Matt 12:38-39). This is the future sign of His death and resurrection (cf. John 2:18-19; 20:31). The fact that Jesus is willing to give them still another sign—and a greater one than all the rest—shows that Jesus still holds on to the hope that some of the religious leaders may yet believe in Him.

This leads to the conclusion that the unpardonable sin is not actually being committed in this passage. Whatever the unpardonable sin actually is, Jesus does not say that the Pharisees *have already committed* it. He simply states that the sin of blasphemy against the Spirit will not be forgiven men. In other words, Jesus is warning them that *if they commit* this sin, it will not be forgiven; that if they continue on the path they are on, the consequences will be irreversible; they will become completely enslaved to their sin, with no hope of rescue.

> Jesus is saying to his antagonists that to attribute to Satan that which has been accomplished by the power and Spirit of God is to demonstrate a moral vision so distorted that there is no longer any hope of recovery. It would be possible to speak against the Son of Man and be forgiven because at that time in Jesus' ministry there was a hiddenness about his person. Not so with the mighty works wrought by the Spirit. They were clear demonstrations that the kingdom (power and reign) of God was present in the world. Denial of this was not the result of ignorance but of a willful refusal to believe.[2]

---

[2] Robert H. Mounce, *Matthew: New International Biblical Commentary* (Peabody, MA: Hendrickson, 1991), 119.

So the Pharisees have not committed this sin. At most, they were *close to committing* the sin and Jesus is issuing a warning to them here. see the full evidence that Jesus was the promised Messiah, but were denying the clear and frequent signs, and explaining these signs away with the unlikely and illogical explanation that the devil was casting demons out of people through Jesus. In Matthew 12:25-30, Jesus shows them how illogical this is. Everyone knows that a house divided against itself cannot stand, and this holds true for the devil's house as well. The evidence that Jesus has provided was more than sufficient to prove He was the Messiah, but the Pharisees cannot accept this truth, and are intent on rejecting Jesus as the Messiah. Craig Keener describes their rejection of Him this way:

> "Blaspheming against the Spirit" here refers specifically to the sin of these Pharisees, who are on the verge of becoming incapable of repentance. The sign of their hardness of heart is their determination to reject *any* proof for Jesus' divine mission, to the extent that they even attribute God's attestation of Jesus to the devil.[3]

Jesus warns that if the religious leaders continue in their unbelief despite all the signs they have seen, it is not He who will be under the power of demons, but they. He says that when a unclean spirit leaves a man, it wanders around looking for a place to live. If it cannot find anywhere, it returns to the place from which it came, and if the house is empty, it moves back in and brings with it seven other spirits more wicked than itself (Matt 12:43-45). Jesus is warning the people that He can only do so much for them. If they do not respond and fill their lives with His presence, then their spiritual sensitivity will be-

---

[3] Craig S. Keener, *A Commentary on the Gospel of Matthew* (Grand Rapids: Eerdmans, 1999), 366.

come worse and worse, until eventually they become a wicked generation which believes the lies of unclean spirits rather than the truth of God.

In the following chapters, Jesus continues to teach and preach about the message of the Kingdom which is being inaugurated in Him, and in numerous instances, Jesus says that His teaching is available for those who have the ears to hear (Matt 13:9, 17, 43). Yet even though many witness His miracles and hear His teachings, He is still rejected by some, and this continued unbelief causes Him to perform fewer and fewer miracles (Matt 13:53-58).

This decreasing frequency of the signs of Jesus seems to solidify in the minds of the religious leaders that Jesus is not a true prophet from God. Yet they continue to ask for more signs (Matt 16:1). Jesus tells them that they are becoming that wicked generation which He warned them about previously (Matt 16:2-4; cf. 12:43-45), but reminds them again that there is still one more sign which He will give to them, the sign of Jonah. Jesus continues to hold out hope that when they see Him risen from the dead, they will accept Him as the Messiah and believe in Him for eternal life.

It is immediately after this that Jesus warns His disciples about the teachings of the Jewish religious leaders, and in which Peter confesses that Jesus is indeed the promised Jewish Messiah for which they have all been waiting (Matt 16:5-20). While some in Israel do not believe, others recognize Jesus for who He is.

THE WORD *BLASPHĒMIA*

One of the key issues in understanding Matthew 12:31-32 is the nature of *blasphemy*. If "blasphemy against the Spirit" will not be forgiven, we must determine what this *blasphemy* is. The Greek word used for *blasphemy is blasphēmia.*

You may notice that the words look and sound almost identical. This is because English is a hybrid language which pulls words from numerous different sources. *Blasphemy* is one of the words English borrowed from Greek. This is nice for Bible translators because then they do not have to translate the word, but it is not nice for people who are trying to understand what the word means, especially when the word is used in a difficult verse like Matthew 12:31.

So the way to understand the word is to look at other contexts where the word is used, both in Scripture and in other Greek literature. When we do that, we find that the word is often translated "revile" and basically means "to speak against" or "abusive speech."[4] The emphasis is on making a judgment about someone, so that *blasphēmia* could be translated as "a reviling judgment." It is almost a condemnation of someone or something else.

That this is a good definition is proven by the parallel statements by Jesus. He essentially says the same exact thing in verse 32 as He said in verse 31, but uses slightly different words. Jesus uses Hebrew parallelism to allow the second statement to further explain and expand upon the first. Arranging them in parallel helps reveal that *blasphemy,* or "reviling judgment," is defined in the context by the phrase "speaking against."

---

[4] Herman Wolfgang Beyer, "*blasphēmeō*" in Gerhard Kittel, ed. *Theological Dictionary of the New Testament* (Grand Rapids: Eerdmans, 1991), I:621-625; Frederick William Danker, ed., *A Greek-English Lexicon of the New Testament and Other Early Christian Literature,* 3rd ed. (Chicago: University of Chicago, 2000), 178.

Matthew 12:31	Matthew 12:32
Every sin and reviling judgment will be forgiven	Anyone who speaks against the Son of Man will be forgiven
A reviling judgment will not be forgiven.	Whoever speaks against the Holy Spirit will not be forgiven.

This definition of blasphemy as a "reviling judgment" is supported elsewhere in Scripture where the word is used.

OTHER SCRIPTURES ABOUT *BLASPHĒMIA*

By itself, the word says nothing about the target of such reviling speech. Although most believe that blasphemy is a sin that can only be committed against God, in various contexts we find that *blasphēmia* can be spoken against other people (cf. Matt 15:19; Eph 4:31; Col 3:8; 1 Tim 6:4) and against the Word of God (Titus 2:5). One surprising use of the word is where the angel Michael refused to blaspheme or revile the devil (Jude 9). One does not often think that the devil can be blasphemed, but the word is used in connection with him. This makes sense when we think of *blasphēmia* as "speaking against" someone, or making a "reviling judgment" about them. The angel Michael refused to make a reviling judgment about the fallen angel Lucifer. He refused to blaspheme Satan. So *blasphēmia* is a reviling judgment made against other humans, the Bible, Satan, or God Himself.

When we look at literature other than the New Testament, we find similar usage. For example, in the Septuagint, which is the Greek translation of the Hebrew Bible, the word is used in 2 Kings 19:4-22 for when the Assyrian ambassador proclaimed a message against the God of Israel within hearing of the walls of Jerusalem. In Daniel

3:29, King Nubuchadnezzar makes it illegal and punishable by death to blaspheme or speak against the God of Shadrach, Meshach, and Abednego. The word is also used in Isaiah 52:5 where God says that the people of Babylon are blaspheming Him continually every day, and as a result, He is going to rescue and redeem His people from captivity.

These Old Testament texts help shed light on what God does in response to blasphemy. In 2 Kings 19 and Isaiah 36, the Assyrian ambassador blasphemes God within hearing of the walls of Jerusalem. This is a clear example of someone speaking against God, and it is because of this speech that God changed His mind about what He was going to do to Assyria.

The series of events which lead up to this blasphemy begin in Isaiah 10:5-6, where God spoke through the prophet Isaiah to announce judgment upon the people of Israel for their many sins. God said that He was going to send Assyria against the people of Israel "to seize the spoil, to take the prey, and to tread them down like the mire of the streets." Several chapters later, the Assyrian army arrives to do just that. And apparently, the Assyrian commander had heard of the prophecy that Israel would fall before his army, and became overly proud, zealous, and confident (Isa 36:10).

This Assyrian commander decided not only to announce his victory over Israel, but to proclaim that through this victory the gods of Assyria were proving that they were more powerful than the God of Israel (Isa 36:20). He threw into their faces the promises that God had made to them about each one sitting under their own fig tree and drinking from their own water cistern (1 Kings 4:25; Micah 4:4; Zech 3:10), and said that the King of Assyria would provide this instead (Isa 36:16).

God became angry that the tool of His wrath, which He sent to carry out His discipline on His people had instead

become so proud that he reviled and blasphemed God
Himself. As a result, God decided to reject and destroy
the Assyrian army, rather than let it carry out the job of
destroying Israel (Isa 37:22-38). The Assyrian blasphemy
against God had serious and dire consequences for the
Assyrian army and the Assyrian king. Rather than being
used by God to accomplish God's will against Israel, the
Assyrians themselves were destroyed.

A similar example is found in Isaiah 52:1-6. God says
that previously, Israel had become the captives of Egypt
and Assyria "without cause" (52:4). This does not mean
that Israel had not sinned and so their captivity was without cause. Instead, it means that Israel had done nothing
to Egypt and Assyria to make them enslave Israel, and so
God delivered Israel from these two nations. The same is
true, God says, of Babylon. Israel had done nothing
against Babylon, and yet Babylon came in and captured
and enslaved God's people. Not only that, but now Babylon was making the people of God wail and suffer in their
captivity, and was continually blaspheming the name of
God every day (52:5).

In these examples from the Hebrew Scriptures, people
are speaking against God in a false and deceitful way.
What they say about Him is so serious, God views it as a
challenge to His honor. In response to their blasphemy,
He reverses their fortunes, frustrates their plans, and in
some cases, has them put to death for making such a
judgment against God. God reverses His original plan and
desire for these nations, and judges them instead. Though
the Assyrian ambassador had power and might on His
side, God defeated him and destroyed his army because
he blasphemed God. Similarly, when the Babylonians
blasphemed God, He rescued Israel from them and sent
invaders to destroy their land.

Note that this does not mean that as a result of their
blasphemy, all the people of Assyria and Babylon were

eternally condemned. To the contrary, God actually promises to bless, deliver, and rescue some of their people. Take the people of Babylon as an example. God says that as a result of their blasphemy, He will rescue and redeem the Israelites out of Babylon (Isa 53–55), and He will also rescue and deliver Babylonian Gentiles who wish to serve God (Isa 56). Their blasphemy does not block them from receiving God's offer of deliverance, forgiveness, and salvation. So in these cases, blasphemy against God resulted in physical death and punishment, but not necessarily eternal death and punishment. God still offered forgiveness and restoration to those who had blasphemed Him.

Nevertheless, it could be argued that all of these Old Testament passages are examples of blasphemy against God the Father, and are not exactly the same thing as blasphemy against the Holy Spirit. While a Trinitarian argument could be made that to blaspheme one member of the Trinity is to blaspheme every member, Jesus Himself sees a distinction between speaking a word of blasphemy against Himself, and speaking a word of blasphemy against the Holy Spirit. He says that every blasphemy against the Son of Man will be forgiven,[5] but blasphemy against the Holy Spirit will never be forgiven.

With all of this context and background information to help guide us, we are now able to look at the primary question: What is the Unforgivable Sin?

---

[5] The phrase "Son of Man" is a favorite term of Jesus. By using it, He is referring primarily to Himself, but includes all humanity with Him. When Jesus uses this phrase as a title for Himself, it is as if He was saying, "I, as the head of the new human race."

WHAT IS THE
UNFORGIVABLE SIN?

Jesus says that every sin will be forgiven, even blasphemy against Himself. Divorce, adultery, abortion, and suicide were discussed in chapter 2, and all fall under the category of "every sin" that will be forgiven. The only sin that will not be forgiven is blasphemy against the Holy Spirit, or speaking against the Holy Spirit.

So what does it mean to speak against the Holy Spirit? In chapter 3 we learned that blasphemy against the Holy Spirit could be defined as speaking a reviling judgment against the Holy Spirit, but this does not really help us understand what the sin *is*. In other words, what does it *mean* to speak a reviling judgment against the Holy Spirit? How does one know whether or not they have committed this sin? How can one protect themselves from committing it? It is to these questions we now turn.

From the context of Matthew 12, it appears that the blasphemy against the Holy Spirit is committed when a person says something which is in complete contradiction and confrontation to what God has said through the Holy Spirit. But it must be more serious than just disagreeing with God (as almost everyone does this at one time or another). It seems to be a type of sin which God takes as a challenge and affront to His honor, and specifically to what God is saying and doing through the Spirit. This sin is so grievous to God, it forces Him to take action against the person who commits it so that God can be found truthful, and every man a liar (Rom 3:4).

But nobody has perfect thoughts and ideas about God and His Word. Does this mean that whenever we mistakenly (or knowingly) say something incorrect about God, we are guilty of committing the unforgivable sin? No. The unforgivable sin is a special type of sin, which can only be committed by certain people in certain circumstances. But what are these circumstances? There are numerous theories as to what these circumstances are and what the blasphemy is which cannot be forgiven. Let us look at some of the more common theories, and analyze these theories based on what we have seen from the previous chapter about the text and context of Matthew 12:31-32.

DENYING CHRIST

Some believe that the blasphemy against the Holy Spirit is a verbal denial of Jesus Christ. It is true that some sort of denial is taking place by religious leaders when they accuse Jesus of performing His miracles by the power of the devil. Many also find support for this view in the statement by Paul from 2 Timothy 2:12 where he writes, "If we deny *Him*, He will also deny us."

Yet there are numerous problems with this view. First, the concept of "denying Christ" is quite vague. What constitutes a denial of Christ, and what does not? How would one know when they have denied Christ? Do they have to say the words, "I deny Christ"? Do words have to be spoken at all? Could denial be some sort of action or thought?

Secondly, the most famous example of someone who rejected and denied Christ is Peter. He even used profanity and curses in denying any connection to Jesus Christ. Yet we know that he was forgiven by Jesus. If denial of Christ was the unpardonable sin, then certainly Peter was guilty of it, and yet we all fully expect to see Peter in heaven.

Third, while the passage in 2 Timothy 2 does say that God will deny us if we deny Him, it also says that if we are faithless, He remains faithful, for He cannot deny Himself. In other words, whatever the denial of 2 Timothy 2:12 is, it is not taking eternal life from someone who already has it, for this would amount to God denying Himself, which He cannot do.

Fourth, denial of Christ doesn't even fit the context here, since such a denial would be a blasphemy against Jesus, which He says will be forgiven. If blasphemy is actually a form of denial (which I think it is), it would have to be against the Holy Spirit. So the unforgivable sin cannot be denying Christ. It must be some sort of sin specifically against the Holy Spirit. But which sort of sins might one commit against the Holy Spirit which would qualify as blasphemy?

CURSING THE HOLY SPIRIT

While there are various sins listed in Scripture as sins against the Holy Spirit, such as grieving and quenching the Spirit (Eph 4:30; 1 Thess 5:19), the sin of blasphemy against the Spirit is the only one which will not be forgiven. Quenching and grieving the Holy Spirit are basically a denial of what the Spirit is doing or a refusal to participate in His work, which means blasphemy against the Spirit must be more serious than these. Since Jesus equates blasphemy of the Spirit with speaking against the Spirit, many argue that the unforgivable sin is cursing the Holy Spirit.

This view is more likely than the previous view, since at least in this view, the sin is against the Holy Spirit rather than against Jesus. But what constitutes a curse? It is more than just being angry at someone, or calling them bad names. A curse is when one person wishes or expresses a desire that some sort of adversity, calamity, or misfortune would fall upon someone else. We have already seen that blasphemy is best defined as "a reviling judgment" which is not the same thing as a curse. Furthermore, there is no hint anywhere in Matthew 12:31-32 of anybody cursing the Holy Spirit. Thus, cursing the Holy Spirit is not the unpardonable sin, because there is no hint of anyone in the context committing this sin, or even thinking of doing so. In fact, most Jewish people at that time did not even believe in the Holy Spirit, so how could they curse Him?[1] They couldn't. So cursing the Holy Spirit is not what Jesus had in mind when He spoke about the blasphemy against the Holy Spirit.

ATTRIBUTING THE WORK
OF THE HOLY SPIRIT TO THE DEVIL

Many believe that the sin of blasphemy against the Holy Spirit is not just cursing the Holy Spirit, but the specific judgment of attributing the works of the Holy Spirit to the works of the devil. In the context, some of the religious

---

[1] If few people believed in the Spirit, why was Jesus warning them about blasphemy against the Spirit? Jews did not believe in the Holy Spirit in a Trinitarian sense the way we do, as the third person of the Trinity. But they did understand God as a spiritual being, and that is how they would have understood Jesus' words. They would have understood Jesus to be speaking about the Spirit of God. Through later revelation we understand that Jesus was speaking of the Holy Spirit, the third person of the Trinity.

rulers state that Jesus was casting out demons by Beelzebub, the ruler of demons (12:24).

So this leads to one of the most popular views about the unpardonable sin, that it is committed when a person sees a work of God, and specifically a miraculous work of the Spirit, and rather than give glory to God for what was done, gives credit to the devil instead. It is believed that this sin is committed when people see the works and miracles of God, but state that the miracles are being performed by the power of Satan rather than by the power of God.

This view is commonly held in Pentecostal charismatic circles where miracles, healings, and demonic exorcisms are a frequent occurrence. Leaders of these ministries argue that when others write off supernatural healings, demonic exorcisms, and the gift of tongues as possibly coming from the devil, such people deny the power of the Holy Spirit, and commit blasphemy against the Holy Spirit.

Of course, in some charismatic circles, the behavior goes way beyond healing and prophecy and speaking in tongues. Some churches engage in holy laughter, barking like dogs and braying like donkeys, getting slain in the Spirit, rolling in the isles, and having tooth fillings changed to gold. When non-charismatic Christian leaders argue that these sorts of activities are unbiblical and therefore not of God, they are condemned by charismatic leaders for being guilty of blasphemy against the Holy Spirit.

Though this is a popular view, it is not the best interpretation of Matthew 12:31-32. First, Scripture is clear that not everything that appears spiritual is from the Holy Spirit. Satan can and does counterfeit the work of God. So we are supposed to test the spirits and see if they are from God (1 John 4:1). If we are convinced a certain activity is not from God but is a counterfeit deception from the devil, it is our obligation to denounce it. It does not seem that God would tell us to test the spirits and denounce those that were false if doing so could accidentally cause some one to commit blasphemy against the Spirit. This warning of Jesus against this sin indicates that one commits it intentionally, not accidentally.

Furthermore, many religions and cults other than Christianity see miracles, signs, wonders, speaking in tongues, ecstatic experiences, dreams, visions, healings, and other such things. Certainly charismatics would be quick to denounce these practices as not being from the Holy Spirit, but since these practices are nearly identical in form and frequency as in charismatic circles, how can they be certain that in condemning these practices in other religions, they are not in fact attributing to the devil a work of the Holy Spirit? God works in mysterious ways, and we cannot be certain that the Holy Spirit is not at work in the lives of other religious practitioners—even in miraculous ways—with the intent of bringing them to faith in Jesus Christ. If charismatics are right, they must not condemn any miraculous utterance, prophecy, sign, miracle, answer to prayer, or spiritual experience of any person or religious group as being of the devil, for there is no way to be certain when and where the Holy Spirit is blowing (John 3:8).

So although this theory is compelling and seems to fit the context of Matthew 12:31-32, the fact that it is impossible to live out in real life indicates that it is not the proper understanding. Theology must not only fit with Scripture, but must also fit with what can be lived out in life.

But aside from even the impracticality of this view, it does not actually fit the context of Matthew 12:31-32 as well as we might initially presume. While it is undoubtedly true that in the context of Matthew 12:31-32, Jesus is performing miracles and casting out demons, and the Pharisees accuse Jesus of doing such things by the power of Beelzebub, this does not mean that condemning the work of the Holy Spirit as a work of the devil *is* the same as blasphemy against the Holy Spirit. As noted in the previous chapter, Jesus does not actually say that the religious leaders have committed the unpardonable sin, but rather were on the path to committing it. If they had already committed it, why would Jesus warn them about it?

So attributing the work of the Holy Spirit to the devil is not the unpardonable sin. Though the Pharisees do make such an accusation against Jesus, He is simply warning them that if they continue on the path they are on, they may *likely commit* the unpardonable sin. They have not committed it yet, but if they persist in denying all the evidence that is before them, they may come to a place where they are beyond the reach of God's grace and forgiveness.

ISRAEL'S NATIONAL REJECTION OF THE MESSIAH

Since the controversy in Matthew 12 involves Jesus defending His claim to be the Messiah to the religious and national leaders of Israel, some Bible scholars and teachers believe that the unpardonable sin is Israel's national rejection of Jesus as the Messiah.

The strength of this view is that it does not simply look at what is said and done in the text of Matthew 12:31-32, but looks at the surrounding context of Matthew 12 and the Gospel of Matthew as a whole, and sees that Jesus is trying to show the people of Israel that He is their promised and prophesied Messiah, but no matter what He says or what miracles He performs, they keep rejecting the truth and denying the clear evidence in the signs that He performs. It is also argued that Matthew 12 is somewhat the turning point in the Gospel of Matthew. From this point on, Jesus begins to minister more toward Gentiles than to Jews (cf. Matt 13–15). Those who hold this view believe that while Jesus came primarily to the Messiah for the Jewish people, after they rejected Him, He refocused His mission toward being the Savior of the world. Matthew 12 is seen as a key text for this transition.

Those who hold this view point out that after the Pharisees claim that Jesus is performing miracles by the power of Satan (12:24), Jesus calls them an "evil generation" which deserves condemnation for rejecting the Messiah (12:39-42). After this, Jesus makes several predictions about how God will turn to a people who will not reject Him, and how Jerusalem and the Temple will be destroyed (cf. Matt 13:41-43; 16:1-4; 21:18-19, 42-46; 22:1-14; 24:1-2).

Note that if this theory is correct, then nobody is able to commit this sin except for the Jewish people living at the time of Jesus Christ. In other words, since we are not Jewish and we are not living at the time of Jesus, we cannot commit this sin. It was a particular sin which only Jewish people could commit who were alive during the ministry of Jesus and who saw the signs He was performing and should have recognized Him as their Messiah, but rejected Him instead.

This view is comforting since it makes the unpardonable sin impossible to commit today. However, this is also the major weakness of the view. While Scripture does at times include descriptions of unique sins that cannot be committed by future generations—such as God's instruction to Adam to not eat fruit from the Tree of the Knowledge of Good and Evil—it does not seem that this particular sin falls into that category. It seems that Matthew included this instruction from Jesus not simply to explain what happened to the Jewish people, but because the possibility of committing this sin is a real danger for all future generations as well. At the time of writing, Matthew was warning his readers about this sin, and people today must receive this warning as well.

Furthermore, the very words of Jesus indicate a warning for all future generations. He applies the warning to "anyone" and not just to the Jewish people who were alive in His day. Jesus also says that anyone who speaks against the Son of Man will be forgiven, but this view about Israel's rejection of Jesus seems to say the opposite, that Jewish people who rejected Jesus by speaking against Him would not be forgiven. So for these reasons, we can say that the unforgivable sin is not Israel's national rejection of Jesus as the Messiah.

FAILURE TO BELIEVE IN JESUS FOR ETERNAL LIFE

A sixth view about the nature of the unpardonable sin is that it occurs when someone fails to believe in Jesus for eternal life. The idea behind this view is that while God forgives all sin, He cannot and will not forgive a person for refusing to believe in Jesus *until* they actually believe in Jesus for eternal life. If they continue in their unbelief until death, then they will never be forgiven, and will therefore be eternally separated from God. Of course, once a person believes in Jesus for eternal life, they are forgiven of this sin as well, and will spend eternity with God.

I held this view for many years, but eventually rejected it for several reasons. First, Jesus says that those who commit this sin will *never* be forgiven. It is not that they might be forgiven if they eventually believe in Jesus, but that once this sin is committed, it will never be forgiven. To say that it will never be forgiven as long as they don't believe removes all the force from Jesus' warning, and makes His argument redundantly self-evident.

Secondly, if Jesus was simply talking about the sin of unbelief, why didn't He just talk about unbelief? He frequently warns people about their lack of faith, so if that was the issue here, why not make the same warning again?

Finally, the big problem with this view is that it once again has almost nothing to do with the Holy Spirit. The concern of Jesus in this particular text is that the unpardonable sin is *against* the Holy Spirit. If a particular view about this sin can be explained without ever mentioning the Holy Spirit, this is a good indication that this view is wrong.

So we must reject this view also. The unpardonable sin is not a failure to believe in Jesus for everlasting life.

WHAT IS THE UNFORGIVABLE SIN?

Ultimately, only one sin fits all of the requirements as the identification of the unforgivable sin. It is this: The unforgivable sin is a willful and slanderous rejection of the Holy Spirit's testimony about Jesus Christ.

This sin fits the text of Matthew 12:31-32 as well as the surrounding context. It fits the words and actions of the Pharisees as well as the words and actions of Jesus. It enables the unpardonable sin to be something that could be committed at the time of Jesus and also today. It maintains the strengths of all the previous views discussed so far in this book, while avoiding the weaknesses. Most importantly, this sin is specifically committed against the Holy Spirit.

Though many do not realize it, the Holy Spirit is actively at work not just in the lives of believers, but also among unbelievers. The Spirit is at work in the world convicting unbelievers of sin, their need for righteousness, and reminding them about the coming judgment (John 16:7-11). The Holy Spirit testifies about Jesus and draws people to Jesus (John 15:26). Without this drawing work of the Holy Spirit upon unbelievers, nobody would ever believe in Jesus for eternal life.

If a person is being convinced by the Holy Spirit that Jesus is the Messiah, is being drawn to Jesus by the Spirit, and is being shown who Jesus is and that judgment is coming if they do not believe in Jesus, and yet that person lashes out verbally at the Holy Spirit, making a "reviling judgment" about what they are being shown, it is then that they commit blasphemy against the Holy Spirit.

There are various forms this willful and verbal rejection of the Spirit might take, but when it is committed by someone, the Holy Spirit backs away from this person forever. The Spirit never returns to them to convict them of sin, righteousness, and judgment. The Spirit stops trying to draw such a person toward faith in Jesus. And when a person no longer is being convicted, convinced, or drawn by the Holy Spirit, they will never believe in Jesus. There is no more hope for them. They are eternally condemned.

HOW DOES A PERSON COMMIT THE UNFORGIVABLE SIN?

What sort of things might cause the Spirit to back away permanently from a person in such a way? It is hard to say with certainty since there are no real examples of it in Scripture. Remember that Jesus does not say that the Jewish religious leaders had committed this sin. No, He is warning them against the sin, hoping that they would not continue down the path they were on. They were refusing the clear signs and teachings of Jesus which should have proven to them that Jesus was the Messiah. They were saying that He was from the devil and that His signs were Satanic. Such words themselves were not the sin of blasphemy against the Spirit, but indicated that they were on the path toward committing such a sin.

The Pharisees clearly saw the signs which Jesus presented, and even asked for more signs, but despite the evidence that was right before their eyes, continued to reject and deny that Jesus was from God, that Jesus was the promised Messiah of Israel. Jesus warned them that if they continued in this manner, they would not be forgiven of this sin. Every other sin would be forgiven them, but not this sin.

So if someone today willfully, scornfully, and slanderously rejects the clear evidence that is laid before them about Jesus and their need to believe in Him for eternal life, and they do this repeatedly, while we can never say with certainty that they have committed the unpardonable sin, we can warn them as Jesus does here that if they continue on that path, they will commit blasphemy against the Spirit, for which there is no forgiveness, and from which there is no return.

In other words, the sin of blasphemy against the Holy Spirit is different than resistance against the Holy Spirit (Acts 7:51). Resisting the Holy Spirit is *a step toward* blasphemy against the Spirit, but is not the same thing. When unbelievers resist the Holy Spirit, they are trying to ignore what the Holy Spirit is telling them about Jesus Christ. They may even attempt to drown out the Spirit's still small voice with other things in life, such as arguments against the existence of God, constant music, recreation, and entertainment, or sex, alcohol, and drugs. They deny the voice of the Spirit which tells them that they have sinned against God and judgment is coming, and believe instead that they are "pretty good" people. If this sounds like nearly every person you know, this is because nearly every unbeliever spends a lot of time and energy resisting the Holy Spirit.

From this state of resisting the Spirit, one of three things will happen. First, an unbeliever may get tired of always resisting the Spirit and may lash out in anger and blasphemy against the Holy Spirit for what He is trying to tell them. The fact that they lash out in such a way proves that they recognized what He was trying to do in their life, but knowingly and maliciously reject it. They completely and utterly refuse "to respond to the overtures of the Spirit of God."[2] They slander the Holy Spirit for His efforts to draw them to Jesus and utterly reject the free offer of eternal life. When this happens, they commit blasphemy against the Holy Spirit. Blasphemy against the Spirit is "a conscious and wicked rejection of the saving power and grace of God towards man. Only the man who sets himself against forgiveness is excluded from it."[3]

The result is that the Holy Spirit stops trying to convict them of sin, righteousness, and judgment. He stops trying to draw them. They have once and for all chosen their path of rebellion against God. Such people demand to be left alone, and the Holy Spirit honors their request.

When an unbeliever lashes out in this way, this reveals a heart hardened beyond hope of forgiveness. They will never be forgiven because they have caused the Holy Spirit to withdraw from them completely. The Holy Spirit stops attempting to convict and convince such people about the truth, love, grace, and mercy found in Jesus Christ. And without the Holy Spirit's work in this way, no person will ever believe in Jesus for eternal life.

Though there is no way to be certain, the numbers of people who commit this sin are probably very small. It is much more likely that the vast majority of people who do

---

[2] Robert H. Mounce, *Matthew: New International Biblical Commentary* (Peabody, MA: Hendrickson, 1991), 119.

[3] Herman Wolfgang Beyer, "*blasphēmeō*" in Gerhard Kittel, ed. *Theological Dictionary of the New Testament* (Grand Rapids: Eerdmans, 1991), I:624.

not believe in Jesus for eternal life never commit the unpardonable sin, but simply die in a state of unbelief and
life-long resistance to the convicting work of the Holy
Spirit. This is the second option for how people may respond to the work of the Spirit. He works tirelessly on
them all the way up until they take their last breath. Such
an unbeliever continues to resist the Holy Spirit throughout his or her life (Acts 7:51; Rom 1:18-20). They never
commit the unpardonable sin, but nor do they ever believe
in Jesus for eternal life. Instead, they live their entire lives
resisting the Holy Spirit and as a result, end up in eternal
separation from God because they never believed in Jesus
for eternal life.

The third and final option is the most desirable. It is
what the Holy Spirit is working toward. While some people may commit the unpardonable sin and the Holy Spirit
stops working on them completely, and others may continue to resist the Holy Spirit their entire lives, there are
many people who will recognize the truth of what the Holy Spirit is showing them, will stop resisting His work,
and will believe in Jesus for eternal life.

This may happen when a person is very young, or only
a second or two before death, but all such people recognize the truth of the Holy Spirit's testimony that we are
sinners, that God is righteous, that judgment is coming,
and the only way to obtain God's righteousness and thus
avoid judgment is to believe in Jesus for eternal life.

Once a person believes in Jesus in this way, they are
born again into God's family and are eternally identified
as one of His children. The possibility of committing the
unpardonable sin is now past because the Holy Spirit has
ceased attempting to draw them to Jesus, and will now
begin to shape and form this new believer into who God
wants them to be. This is the subject of the next chapter.

WHY YOU HAVE NOT COMMITTED THE UNFORGIVABLE SIN

Based on what we have learned in this book, it can be said with confidence that if you are concerned about committing the unforgivable sin, this is proof that you have not committed it.

Do you understand why?

The unpardonable sin is committed when a person knowingly and maliciously lashes out against the Holy Spirit. This sin is so terrible, it causes the Holy Spirit to stop convicting and convincing such a person about sin, righteousness, and judgment. The Holy Spirit will no longer draw such a person to Jesus.

Therefore, anyone who has committed the unpardonable sin *does not worry about committing the unpardonable sin*. They don't really care about committing any sin whatsoever. Since the Spirit is no longer convicting such a person of their sin, of God's righteousness, or of the coming judgment, such a person will not be concerned about their sin, will have no fear of God, and will not care about heaven, hell, or what happens after death.

If you are concerned about such things, this is a good sign. It indicates that the Holy Spirit is still working in your life to convict you of sin, teach you about God's righteousness, and remind you of the coming judgment. If you think about these things, and recognize that sin is an affront to God's righteousness, and that judgment is coming for every person on earth, then this means that the Holy Spirit has not abandoned you, and you have not committed the unforgivable sin.

So be encouraged. The simple fact that you are reading this book probably indicates that you are concerned about committing this sin. Reading and wondering about the unforgivable sin is a good indication you have not committed it.

But let me alleviate your concern even further. Many people are fairly certain that they have not yet committed the unforgivable sin, but are worried that they might commit it in the future. Just as you can know that you have not yet committed the unforgivable sin, you can also know that you never will.

You Will Never Commit the Unforgivable Sin

If you have believed in Jesus for eternal life, then you can be confident that you will never commit the unforgivable sin. How can you know this? Because as has already been shown, the unpardonable sin is, by definition, something that only unbelievers can commit.

As was shown in the last chapter, the Spirit is at work in the world convicting unbelievers of sin, their need for righteousness, and reminding them about the coming judgment so that they will believe in Jesus for eternal life. If a person knowingly, willfully, slanderously, repeatedly and verbally rejects what the Holy Spirit is clearly showing them, then there may come a point when the Holy Spirit stops trying to draw this person to believe in Jesus for eternal life and leaves them to their eternal ruin instead.

But once a person believes in Jesus for eternal life, the Spirit's relationship with that person changes forever. No longer does the Spirit try to convince such a person that they need to believe in Jesus, for they have already believed in Him! Instead, once a person believes in Jesus, that person has been regenerated, indwelled, baptized, and sealed by the Holy Spirit (John 3:3; Titus 3:5; John 14:16-17; 1 Cor 12:13; Eph 1:13-14). The Spirit's task is now to empower this person live according to the rule and reign of the Kingdom of God so that they look, act, and think more like Jesus Christ. In other words, the task of the Spirit towards unbelievers is radically different than the task of the Spirit toward believers. The unpardonable sin stops the Spirit from performing His task toward unbelievers, but nothing in Scripture talks about anything that will stop the Spirit from performing His task toward believers. While believers can quench what the Spirit is trying to do (1 Thess 5:19), and grieve the Spirit by our sinful rebellion (Eph 4:30), the Spirit will never stop working within us to make us ever more like Jesus.

So if you have believed in Jesus for eternal life, it is no longer possible to commit the unpardonable sin. You have already been drawn to Jesus by the Spirit, and have been convicted of sin, righteousness, and judgment. That aspect of the Spirit's job toward you is finished and complete. He is now working on you in other ways which cannot be stopped by any sort of sin which you might commit. Once you have received eternal life through faith alone in Jesus, it is eternal and cannot be taken away. Once you are in the Father's hands, nothing can take you out (Matt 10:28-29). Nothing in all creation can separate you from God, not even something in your own life (Rom 8:38-39).

CAN GOD REALLY FORGIVE ME?

I opened this book by telling the story of Jamie. She had said and done some pretty bad things in her life and was convinced that she had committed the unpardonable sin. Through our email exchanges, I was able to share with her some of the things I have written about in this book. As we exchanged emails, I found that her real reasons for believing she had committed the unpardonable sin were not the statements of Jesus in Matthew 12:31-32.

Over and over, as I tried to explain to Jamie that she had not committed the unpardonable sin, she said, "Yes, but there is no way God could love me," or "Yes, but you don't know everything I've done. God cannot forgive me." It eventually dawned on me that while Jamie and I had been looking carefully at the text of Matthew 12:31-32 and the various options for understanding that text, what she really needed was a better understanding of God's love and forgiveness. She needed to know that God could love and forgive *her*. It was only when she understood this that she was able to find freedom and deliverance from fear and guilt.

Ever since, whenever someone contacts me about the unpardonable sin, I spend most of my time trying to help them understand the love and forgiveness of God. While I do explain Matthew 12:31-32, I have found that the most important thing they need to know is that God truly loves and forgives them. So let me spend the last few pages of this book trying to show you the same thing.

GOD LOVES YOU

God loves you more than you can ever know. This truth is difficult to accept in a world so full of hate and rejection, but it is precisely because this world is full of hate that God wants you to know how much He loves you. To show this, God sent His only Son, Jesus Christ, to reveal His infinite love to us. So if you want to know how much God loves you, do not look at the problems you are facing in life. Do not look at the hateful and hurtful ways your father treated you. Do not look at how your friends have abandoned you, your children have rejected you, or even how the church has judged and condemned you.

If you want to know what God is like and how much God loves you, just look at Jesus. The Scriptures teach that Jesus is the exact representation of God (Col 1:15), and that Jesus reveals what God is like (John 14:8-11). So to learn about the love of God, read the Gospels and watch Jesus as He spends time with sinners, tax-collectors, and prostitutes. Listen to Him as He tells those who are divorced and caught in adultery that He loves and forgives them (John 4:17-18; 8:1-11). Be amazed at how He loves and forgives Peter after he denied, rejected, slandered, and cursed Jesus (John 21:15-17). As you read the Gospels, note how Jesus never condemns or judges any person, no matter how bad, except for religious leaders who are themselves judging and condemning others.

Ultimately, look at Jesus on the cross. Listen to Him as He freely forgives those who are putting Him to death and lovingly welcomes a condemned thief into paradise (Luke 23:34-43). Reading through the Gospels shows time and time again that Jesus loves and accepts all people. The only people He has harsh words for are those who want to restrict God's love for other people.

The Gospels show us that no matter what you have done, no matter what you have said, Jesus has infinite love for you, and since He shows us perfectly what God is like, you can know that God has infinite love for you as well. You do not have to earn this love or gain this love through good behavior. God loves you no matter what sin you might have committed.

Romans 5:8 says that while we were yet sinners, Christ died for us. Jesus died for us on the cross *because* we were sinners. He didn't die for people who had their lives all fixed up and sorted out. He died for sinners because He loves sinners. If you are grieved and worried about your sin, then be encouraged, for you are just the kind of person Jesus loves.

Never believe the lie that your sin can separate you from the love of God. God is not surprised or shocked by your sin. Remember that when He sent Jesus Christ to this earth, He knew every sin you would ever commit. He knew all your sins before you would ever commit them. And yet He sent Jesus anyway, to die for your sins. This is how much He loves you. God loves you so much that through Jesus Christ, He made your sin a non-issue.

Sin does have consequences, of course. But the consequences of sin are not because God hates or rejects you. If you end up in prison or getting a divorce because of something you did, this does not mean that God has rejected and condemned you forever. No, such things are simply the natural consequences of going against God's instructions for life. The reason God has given instructions about how to live life is not to ruin our joy and destroy our fun, but to make sure we have the best life possible. If we go against what God has said, it should not surprise us when we end up with problems. But these problems are not because God has turned away from you. No, He loves you just as much as He did before you sinned. But just as the laws of nature have cause and effect, so also the spiritual laws of God have effects upon those who break them. If you jump out a window you will fall, and if you treat your wife in an unloving way, you will probably end up with a divorce.

The commands of God liberate us from addictive sin and enable us to enjoy life more fully. The laws of God provide freedom from captivity to sin, and protect us from the destructive consequences of sin.

Sometimes the consequences for our sin are due to the discipline of God. But even still, God's discipline is not because He hates us and wants to condemn us for all eternity, but because He loves us and wants to teach us the right way to live. God disciplines those He loves (Heb 12:6).

The discipline of God upon those who have strayed from His will has nothing to do with a person's eternal life or God's love for that person. It is true that due to prolonged sin and disobedience God may discipline a person through sickness or death, and may even discipline a country through allowing war, famine, and natural disasters to come upon that country. But these forms of discipline never involved the eternal destiny of people. No, with such discipline God is simply trying to bring a person or a country back into the joyous experience of His love, care, and protection.

It is like a parent who disciplines their child. Good and Godly parents train their children so that they can enjoy life and avoid the pain and hardships of life. Sometimes this discipline involves pain to the child or taking away privileges from the child. But in this process, no Godly parent would ever tell their child, "You are no longer my son. You are no longer my daughter. I hate you and want nothing to do with you ever again." Granted, even though such words should never be said, some parents do say these things to their children. But nevertheless, such words cannot *actually* sever the family bond between parent and child? Of course not. Nothing can erase or do away with the fact that those parents had those children. No sin, no matter how grievous, and no words, no matter how hateful, can dissolve the eternal and unbreakable bond between parent and child.

Similarly, the bond between God and one of His children cannot be broken. And unlike some earthly parents, God would never tell one of His children that He hates them and wants nothing to do with them. To the contrary, He said exactly the opposite in the person and work of Jesus Christ. Absolutely nothing can separate us from the love of God, not angels, nor demons, nor even our own words and actions. God's love for you is infinite and eternal. Your sin is not an issue with God, no matter how terrible. Why not? Because out of His great love for you, He has already forgiven all your sin.

GOD HAS ALREADY FORGIVEN YOUR SIN

One of the main problems that causes people to think that God cannot forgive their sin is the mistaken belief that sin is what keeps a person out of heaven. Most people believe today that the difference between people in heaven and people in hell is a matter of morality. It is thought that those who are in heaven are good people, and those in hell are bad.

The Scriptures teach the exact opposite, that all have sinned, that everyone is wicked, and that whether you have committed one sin or one million, everyone is equally guilty before God (Rom 3:23; Jas 2:10).

Many within the Christian church recognize the truth that all are sinners, and yet they still believe that sin is the primary difference between those who have eternal life and those who do not. They state that while all have sinned, and while eternal life is a free gift of God, we are still required to confess and repent of our sin in order to be forgiven. Many churches teach that if a person does not properly repent of their sin, of if they die with unconfessed sin, they will not spend eternity with God in heaven, but will end up in hell. So once again, sin is viewed as the primary thing that separates those in heaven from those in hell.

Once again, the Scriptures teach the exact opposite. Sin is not an issue with God. Sin does not send a person to hell, nor does sin keep a person out of heaven. While it is true that Jesus Christ died on the cross because of sin and for our sin, it is also true that every sin of every person was placed upon Jesus as He died on the cross. When Jesus died, He did away with sin completely. God, in Christ, completely and permanently forgave the sins of all people in the entire world (John 3:16; Heb 9:26-28; 1 Pet 2:24; 3:18; 1 John 2:2).

This means that all of your sins have already been forgiven. Every single one. The sins you have already committed, the sins you are committing, and the sins you have yet to commit—they are forgiven. Therefore, sin is not an issue with God.

The issue with God is righteousness. The thing that distinguishes people who spend eternity with God from those who spend eternity separated from God is whether or not they have the life of God within them. It is not a matter of sin, for that has been removed from us as far as the east is from the west (Ps 103:12). It is a matter of whether or not a person has received God's life.

And how does a person receive God's life? By believing in Jesus for it (John 3:16; 5:24; 6:47; 1 John 5:11-12). Eternal life is not gained simply by believing that Jesus existed or that He died on the cross and rose again. These things are true, but people can believe these things without believing in Jesus *for eternal life*. The life that is in God, the righteous life of God, *eternal life*, is given only to those who believe in Jesus for it. When a person believes in Jesus for eternal life, they are immediately credited with the righteousness of God, are transferred from the kingdom of darkness and brought into the kingdom of light, are given the Holy Spirit to regenerate, indwell, baptize, and seal them, and are joined eternally with the universal family of God. Sin—or the forgiveness of sin—is not the issue; eternal life is. All sins have already been forgiven in Jesus Christ.

Some may object that passages like 1 John 1:9 and Luke 3:3 indicate that confession and repentance are required to receive the forgiveness of sins. Let us briefly consider both of these passages to see what they teach about the forgiveness of God.

FORGIVENESS AND CONFESSION

There is a need for the confession of sins, but not to receive the universal forgiveness of sins in Jesus Christ. This universal and complete forgiveness has already been freely given to all, whether people confess or not. So what does confession do? The confession of sins is needed to help us gain the day-to-day freedom from the power of sin in our lives, and to help maintain our family fellowship with God.

While our relationship with God is eternal and unchanging, our fellowship with God is not. Once again, this is just like any family relationship. A child is always a child of his or her parents no matter what happens and no matter what is said or done. The fellowship between child and parent, however, can be damaged and even ruined. If a child does something which brings deep shame to the family, the parents may disown the child and treat them as if they were dead. The child is still biologically part of the family—nothing whatsoever can change that fact—but such a child will not see other members of the family for holidays and family gatherings. They might not even attend weddings and funerals. The family relationship is still intact, but the family fellowship is so broken that almost nothing can mend and repair it.

So also with the family of God. Before a person is born into the family, God has forgiven all their sins. Though many unbelievers do not recognize they are sinners, Jesus says the same thing about them that He said on the day He was crucified: "Father, forgive them, for they do not know what they do" (Luke 23:34). At the same time, the Holy Spirit is trying to convince them of their sin, of God's righteousness, and of the coming judgment so that they can see how much God loves them and what has been done about their sin in Jesus Christ. He does this in the hopes that they will believe in Jesus for eternal life and gain the righteousness of God.

Once a person believes in Jesus for eternal life, they begin their relationship with God just like any baby begins its relationship with its mother: in perfect harmony and peace. In the case of God's family, the Father and the child are in perfect fellowship. As we remain in fellowship, the blood of Jesus continually purifies us from all sin (1 John 1:7). As new believers, we may not know all that God expects from members of His household. We may not know how to live according to rule and reign of God. As a result, it is probably not long—maybe only a few seconds—before the new believer sins. When this happens, what does God do? God forgives. Repentance and confession are not required because new believers often do not know how to properly behave as a member of the family of God.

I once sat with a new believer who used profanity in his very first prayer. I smiled to myself as I listened to him pray, and I believe God smiled also. Was the bad word a sin? Yes. Was God approving of this man's sin? Of course not. But God is thrilled with every new person who is born into His family no matter how they come to Him.

All of us should be extremely grateful for this. I am convinced that all of us commit numerous sins every day

which we do not realize are sinful. And if we had to specifically confess each one of these sins, we would spend
all day trying to figure out what was sinful and what
wasn't, and confessing anything and everything which
might potentially be sinful, just so that we could make
sure we had confessed everything. Thankfully, we do not
have to do this, because Jesus cleanses us from all sin,
whether we confess it or not.

But there comes a day in the life of every believer
when God decides to start working on us with a particular
sin. There is no set order or timeframe on sins God seeks
to liberate us from. God works with each person in His
own time and His own way. But He does work on each
one of us. God decides that a particular behavior or
thought pattern in our life must change. He wants to make
us look more like Jesus, and help us better reveal the light
of the Gospel, and to do that, we must straighten out a
particular area of our life.

So God instructs the Holy Spirit to begin working on
us in that area. When this happens, God has already forgiven us for this sin. But when we sin, God wants us to
come to Him and admit what we have done, and thank
Him for the forgiveness we have in Jesus Christ. This
helps maintain our fellowship with God.

Once again, it is like any parent-child relationship. If a
child sins against a parent, and the parent asks the child
about it, the worst thing is for the child to deny it. The
child is caught, and denial only compounds the problem.
But if the child confesses what they have done, then the
fellowship between parent and child is maintained. This is
how it works with God as well.

When we sin and God points our sin out to us, we are
faced with a choice. We can either agree that what we are
doing is sinful, and begin to take steps to correct it, or we
can argue with the Holy Spirit and cling to our sinful behavior instead. If we choose to argue with God and say

that what we are doing is not sinful, then we are deceiving ourselves and are choosing lies and falsehood over God's truth (1 John 1:8).

If we choose the route of lies and self-deceit, a small rift opens in our fellowship with God. The relationship stays intact, but our communion with God is slightly damaged. Nothing can damage the relationship, but the fellowship is marred. The longer we argue with God about the sinful behavior in our life, the greater that rift becomes, until one day, the chasm is so wide, there is almost no fellowship with God whatsoever. We never show up for holidays or family gatherings. We keep away from God because by denying that we are sinning, we are calling Him a liar (1 John 1:10).

The other option is to agree with God that we have sinned. When we confess our sins to God in this way, He is faithful and just and reminds us of our forgiveness of sins through the cleansing work of Jesus Christ (1 John 1:9). Through such confession, perfect fellowship continues with God.

None of this, of course, gives us the freedom to sin. To the contrary, understanding the full love and acceptance of God should make us want to please and honor Him even more by not sinning. But if and when we do sin, it is encouraging and comforting to know that Jesus Christ is standing always before the throne of God, saying, "Yes, I died for that sin too. And that one. He is still righteous" (1 John 2:1).

So confession of sin is not the condition by which forgiveness is received. Rather, it is the condition by which fellowship with God is maintained.

FORGIVENESS AND REPENTANCE

What about repentance? Several passages in Scripture seem to indicate that repentance is necessary to receive the forgiveness of sins. For example, in Luke 3:3 we read that John preached a baptism of repentance for the forgiveness of sins. Does this teach that forgiveness is dependent upon repenting and being baptized?

Yes and no. Part of the difficulty with the word "forgiveness" is that modern English speakers have put a slightly different twist on the word than how people would have understood the equivalent Greek or Hebrew words in the Scriptures when they were written. "Forgiveness" doesn't mean exactly the same thing it did 2000 years ago.

The word "forgiveness" today describes a vague, psychological state that exists within the mind of a person. It is kind of like peace or joy. These exist, but they are primarily mental states of being.

The word "forgiveness" comes from the Greek word *aphesis,* and while it can be translated as "forgiveness," it is closer to something like "liberty," "freedom," or "release." It is used of the release of captives and slaves, of the cancellation of debt, or even of divorce (LXX: Isa 61:1; Jer 34:8-17; Ezek 46:17; Matt 6:12; Matt 13:36).[1] So when New Testament authors write about the forgiveness of sins, they have in mind the cancellation of debt or the release of a slave from captivity to sin. Repentance for the forgiveness of sins has nothing to do with gaining eternal life and entering heaven, but about freedom from the captivating and addictive power of sin.

---

[1] Colin Brown, ed., *The New International Dictionary of New Testament Theology* (Grand Rapids: Zondervan, 1971), I:698-701; Rudolf Bultmann, *"aphesis"* in Gerhard Kittel, ed., *Theological Dictionary of the New Testament* (Grand Rapids: Eerdmans, 1964), I:509-512.

This idea fits well with everything we have seen in this book. God wants us to admit that we have sinned, and deal with it, not because sin is a big issue with God, but because He sees how much sin is hurting and damaging us. He wants us to confess our sin so that we can be liberated from it, and released from its addictive power in our lives. Sin damages us, and God reveals our sin to us, not so that He can threaten us with hell if we do not confess and repent, but so that by agreeing with Him that we have sinned (confession), and taking steps to move in the opposite direction (repentance), we can be released (forgiven) from any sin that holds sway over our lives.

FORGIVENESS OF SIN AND THE UNFORGIVABLE SIN

All of this leads back to the question of the unforgivable sin. If God has already forgiven every sin of every person in all the world through the death of Jesus Christ, then how is it that there is one sin that will never be forgiven?

In Matthew 12:31-32, the issue is not about whether or not you have "forgiveness." Through Jesus Christ, God has already forgiven you for all sin. What blasphemy against the Spirit does is throws the forgiveness of God back in His face, saying, "I don't want it, and I never will." In this way, the unforgivable sin is the willful rejection of the forgiveness we already have. The Holy Spirit is trying to teach us about this forgiveness of sin, but when we slanderously reject what the Holy Spirit is telling us about God's love and forgiveness, there comes a point where the Spirit backs away, essentially saying, "Fine. If you want to remain enslaved to sin, go right ahead. I will leave you to it. I tried to show you that Jesus Christ has released you from all your sin, but you want nothing to do with it. So be enslaved. Be captive. Be chained." It is as Robert Mounce has written: "The only sin that God is unable to forgive is the unwillingness to accept forgiveness."[2]

BELIEVE IN JESUS FOR ETERNAL LIFE

So how do you know if you, or a friend, or relative, have committed the unforgivable sin? First, if you have believed in Jesus Christ for eternal life, then it is no longer possible for you to blaspheme the Holy Spirit. Since you have believed in Jesus for eternal life, the Holy Spirit has ceased the work upon you which He performs on unbelievers, and is now living within you to mold and shape you into Christlikeness. Due to this, a Christian can quench and grieve the Holy Spirit, but cannot blaspheme the Spirit in the way Christ talks about in Matthew 12:31-32. If you are a believer, do not worry about committing the unpardonable sin. The possibility of committing this sin is forever in your past.

If, however, you are not a Christian, and worry that you might have committed this sin, be encouraged. Nobody who commits the blasphemy against the Spirit wonders if they have. They no longer care about such things. The unbeliever who commits this sin has become so morally and spiritually blind that their heart is hardened. The Holy Spirit has stopped trying to convince them of sin, righteousness, and judgment. As a result, they have become fully enslaved to sin, to the point that they no longer care about spiritual things and will never believe in Jesus. Such a condition is clearly not true of you, because you are reading this book and are concerned about your spiritual state. This proves that the Holy Spirit is still working on you, and therefore, you have not yet committed the unpardonable sin.

---

[2] Robert H. Mounce, *Matthew: New International Biblical Commentary* (Peabody, MA: Hendrickson, 1991), 119.

But be warned. If you have not yet believed in Jesus for eternal life, then the warning that Jesus gave to the religious leaders may apply to you as well. Jesus told the Pharisees that if they continued to reject the truths which were clearly before their eyes, then there may come a day when the Spirit stops trying to convince them. So if you have not believed in Jesus for eternal life, do not resist the Spirit any longer. There is still time. Do not delay. Receive eternal life and become a member of God's family by believing in Jesus Christ (John 3:16; 5:24; 6:47). Once you have believed in Jesus for eternal life, the possibility of committing the unpardonable sin becomes an impossibility forever.

> If you're afraid you've committed the unpardonable sin, stop worrying. Jesus is not a liar! If you believe in Him for eternal life, then you've got it. It's that simple. He guarantees it.[3]

---

[3] Bob Wilkin, "Christians and the Unpardonable Sin" Grace in Focus Newsletter March-April:1997 (Denton, TX). http://www.faithalone.org/news/y1997/97B2.html Last accessed June 7, 2012.

APPENDIX:
A SAMPLE EMAIL

Below is one of my email exchanges with a person struggling with the unpardonable sin. Though some of my email exchanges on this topic go on for several months (even years!), this is one of the shorter exchanges. I chose to share it because it shows the fear and guilt that people struggle with and how I try to get them to see the love and forgiveness of God in Jesus Christ.

Here is the email I received from "N." about a year ago:

> I don't think you can write me back anything that will give me any kind of peace. I am such a mess. I am sorry to burden you with my horrid case.
>
> I regret being so very sinful. I am terrified. I want to be forgiven.
>
> I don't know if I was ever truly saved before I thought a horrid thought, and my fear of being unpardonable started. Right when I learned there was such a thing as the unpardonable sin, I pretty much thought a terrible thought, and then I was distraught.

I think I said something out loud that was unpardonable.

I feel sick. I am sorry for writing you. I guess I am just wishing there was help for me. Your article seemed very thought out. I probably shouldn't be writing you, because I'm just hopeless.

Note that N. did not know about the unpardonable sin until someone told her about it, and it was then that the fear and guilt set in. Now N. feels completely worthless and hopeless and like nobody can help.

Here is my first response:

Do not be hopeless. God loves you more than you can think or imagine, and has completely forgiven you for every sin, past, present, and future. There is nothing you can say which He has not heard before, and which will offend Him into casting you off forever.

If you believe in Jesus for eternal life, you are adopted into the family of God, and there is no way God will ever "unadopt" you. For some peace, read John 14–16 to see how much Jesus loves you.

I am praying for you, that you will not listen to lies of Satan about how God could never forgive you, and instead listen to the truth of God that He has already forgiven you, and wants to welcome you into His forever family.

You may recognize some of the ideas and themes that have been discussed in this book. Since I am not sure who the person is or what exactly they are struggling with, my answers are quite brief. I am fishing for more information and wanting to see if she is open to further discussion.

Frequently, people who struggle with the unpardonable sin are in very legalistic churches which teach them that God hates them if they sin, and they must live perfect lives to become a child of God. Occasionally when I tell such people that eternal life is given to those who simply believe in Jesus for it, they write back condemning me as a heretic and I never hear from them again. This has only happened two times that I can think of, but I have learned to test the waters with these initial emails before launching into an extended explanation of the unpardonable sin.

In the case of N. it was only a few hours later when I received this reply:

> Oh, I am amazed you wrote me back, and I'm amazed you wrote that to me. Thank you.
>
> I am so afraid. It is hard for me to explain to you how much I fear that I have committed what will never be forgiven. I don't know how to explain it.
>
> If I spoke against the Holy Spirit, how can I ever be forgiven of that?
>
> Jesus said that I will never be forgiven in Matthew 12:32, so I am just terrified and feel hopeless.
>
> I cannot remember what I said out loud. I just remember I was in the bathroom. And I think I was praying and confessing to God a bad thought that I thought, about the Holy Spirit, and I was mumbling my prayer out loud, and then I think I said my bad thought out loud. So then I literally spoke against the Holy Spirit, so I think I'm hopeless.
>
> The problem is, I think I was praying and asking for forgiveness when it happened, but I really don't remember. It happened months ago. I don't remember. I just remember thinking in the bathroom, "Oh no. I think I just spoke against the Holy Spirit." But then I think I told myself, "No, I didn't," and I just let it go. But now I think I'm unpardonable.

Months ago, in the bathroom, I didn't panic or anything. I just went on with my day (feeling guilty and tormented over thinking such a horrid thought... That's how all my days are now, I am always feeling tremendous guilt and dread over thinking something horrid. That is how my life has been for years and years.

What if I said something against the Holy Spirit, and it was not in my mumbled prayer, or in confession, and I'm remembering it wrong? If so, then I'm guilty.

I am just feeling so scared, like I'm guilty of the unpardonable sin, and there is no hope for me. I wish there was forgiveness available to me, but I fear I'm unforgivable.

I am again so thankful for your e-mail, I am going to re-read it many times. And I'll read John 14–16. I'm trying to tell myself hopeful things, like Jesus will not cast me out (John 6:37) but then when I think of Matthew 12:32 then I just think I'm hopeless. I don't want to change God's Word, and think, "Well, it says this, but it really doesn't mean that." It says what it says.

I am so sorry to burden you. I am the most horrid person, and I put myself in this hopeless spot, and I regret it so much, and I'm just a wretched person, I know that. I'm just scared. And I guess looking for help.

I'm thankful you said you are praying for me. That is so kind of you. I do not deserve your kindness or prayers.

I am afraid Jesus said speaking against the Holy Spirit is unforgivable, and so if I'm guilty of that, then I'm hopeless. I think I am guilty of that.

I wish I was never born. I would love to be adopted into God's family and forgiven and saved. I'm sorry for sharing my messed up, hopeless situation, I guess I'm just looking for help.

Sometimes I get a sense that there is a lot more going on in a person's life than just a fear about the unpardonable sin. I sensed this with N. I rarely find out what the issue is, but it could be something like verbal or physical abuse in their marriage or family. If so, they often feel that since their closest loved ones have abandoned and rejected them, then maybe God has too. Sometimes there is psychological issues which need to be addressed. I am not a professional counselor, and counseling through email is impossible, and so when I sense that there are issues which might need professional help, I recommend that the person seek out a competent counselor in their area with whom they can meet and discuss these issues.

In the previous email from N. I sensed that there might be deeper issues which would require professional care, but since N. was asking specifically about Matthew 12:31-32, and could not even remember what was said in the bathroom, I decided to address this question and then see where the conversation went.

> Regarding Matthew 12:32, you wrote that "It says what it says." That is true. The problem, of course, is knowing what it says. Though Matthew 12:32 does say that speaking against the Holy Spirit will not be forgiven, the text does not say what it means to speak against the Holy Spirit. So I can say with confidence that whatever you said in the bathroom about the Holy Spirit or to Him is not what Jesus had in mind in Matthew 12:32.
>
> How do I know? Because if the Holy Spirit had truly departed from you, then you would not be feeling guilty and like you need forgiveness. The Holy Spirit is the one who convicts us of sin, righteousness, and judgment. Since you believe you have sinned (and you probably did), then this

means that the Holy Spirit is convicting you of it. That is good news!

If the Holy Spirit is convicting you, then He did not leave you forever, which means you did not commit the unpardonable sin. Instead, you probably just committed some other sin. So confess it to God, and He will cleanse you, and purify you of all sin (1 John 1:9). And then let Him tell you how much He loves you and wants to teach you about Himself through Scripture.

You are not a wretched and horrid person. God loves you infinitely. You matter to Him. And to me.

I hope this helps a little bit.

Again, I do not give a long, theological explanation. I am not sure how much N. knows about God and Scripture, and do not want to send a 10,000 word email trying to explain the text and context of Matthew 12:31-32. I just want to summarize the view presented in this book and see what sort of response I get. My goal, as always, is to gently lead and direct a person to read in Scripture for themselves about the love and forgiveness of God in Jesus Christ.

This next email is actually a combination of N.'s last email to me, interspersed with my reply.

>>>N., my reply is inserted into your email. My wife helped me write this email as well, as she shows the love of God better than anyone I know. Our comments are preceded with these marks: >>>

I am very thankful for your kindness. Thank you very, very, very much for e-mailing me that. It has brought me some relief. I am just, sorry to say, still so worried about it. I'm just so afraid.

>>>Fear is from Satan. That is his greatest tactic. Run from it. God is love.

I hope so very whole heartedly that because I am feeling convicted of my sin, I hope that means I am not guilty of the unpardonable sin. I hope I really didn't commit the unpardonable sin.

>>>You didn't commit it. You are no more guilty than the rest of us.

Does it matter the tense of the word "speaks" in Matthew 12:32? Could that mean, if you are speaking against, then you will never be forgiven, because you are being against the Lord and not surrendering and accepting His forgiveness, but if you turn from that, you can be forgiven? I don't know. I was thinking, it doesn't say, if you "spoke" against, it says "speaks," right? Does that make a difference? I am just afraid I did "speak" against the Holy Spirit, and it was unpardonable, and I'm just terrified.

>>>I am happy to discuss theology and Scripture, but at some point we just need to remember who God is at His core. He is love. He is full of grace, kindness, and mercy. He loves you. He loves you so very much, and it is breaking His heart that you are in pain over this.

I am just trying not to think or fret. That is hard to do. I have asked the Lord for mercy and forgiveness. I agree with Him that I sinned against Him, and I was so sinful and terrible, and I turned from my sin, and I never want to do it again. That is confessing and repenting, right? I wish I never thought terrible thoughts, or said anything sinful. I regret being so sinful.

>>>You are forgiven. God says to you, "I love you my child." That is what He is saying to you right now, and has always been saying to you. Jesus didn't die on the cross so

that He could hold sin over us and condemn us. No, He died on that cross so that we could understand and see how very much He loves us. He loves you, N.

I wish I was never born.

>>>Please don't say that, because God made you to walk this earth for a designated time and He doesn't make mistakes. But you can't fully live for Him if you are letting Satan keep you in the grip of fear. Whatever you did, it is forgiven. I don't care what you said, it is forgiven in Jesus Christ. Maybe what you said truly was horrible, but trust me when I say that it is forgiven. That is the whole point of Christ's death. He died for all of us, because He loves us so very much. He loves you N. He loves You. He died for you. You are forgiven.

I am sorry to burden you with this, I just found your article online. I don't even know if you are a pastor or counselor, but I am so thankful you have taken time to kindly and thoughtfully write me. I want you to be correct, that if I am feeling convicted by the Holy Spirit, then He did not leave me forever, and I did not commit the unpardonable sin.

>>>You are not a burden; you are a living testimony of God's love. So go be that love to others. Be a testimony of God's love. Go out and live like you have been forgiven. Live like you are loved by the highest King ever. Live like you have forever to live. Live like you don't care about what anybody says except God. Live like someone died for you, and has forgiven you. Because someone has, and His name is Jesus.

I want to have peace with God, and be forgiven and loved by Him.

>>>Listen to what God is saying to you in John 14:27: "Peace I leave with you, My peace I give to you; not as the world gives do I give to you. Let not your heart be troubled, neither let it be afraid." When you forgive yourself you will find peace, God has already forgiven you.

Thank you for writing me. Thank you for telling me God loves me infinitely. I want to believe that, I think if I committed the unpardonable sin, how can He love me? In John 3:16, it says, "For God so loved the world..." So people in the world, in the past, have committed the unpardonable sin, but God says He loved the world, so did He love the people that committed the unpardonable sin and does He still love them? Does He still love me? If I am guilty of the unpardonable sin, will He still love me in some type of way? I am afraid He doesn't love me because I'm unpardonable, and He won't or cannot forgive me, because I'm unpardonable. But I'm trying to not think like that.

>>>Do you truly believe deep down that you serve a loving and kind God, a God that was willing to die for you, a God that loves you so much He gave up everything to come down to earth to show you how much He loves you? Because if you do there is no way that you could think that you are in trouble. He has already forgiven you and He loves you so much. He wants you to go and live for Him, shining His light in this dark world. And in fact, feeling as low as you do might be helpful in that you can understand what so many other people in this world are going through. You can come alongside others who think God does not love them, and show them what you have learned, that God loves all of us more than we can ever imagine.

I think I am the worst sinner in the world, in a totally hopeless situation, and I'm sorry for burdening you with all of this. I am sorry. I'm trying to think calmly without panicking, that maybe I'm not guilty of the unpardonable sin. I am thankful you wrote me such kind things, I do not deserve such kindness. I am very thankful that you took time to write me such hopeful things, thank you. And sorry for all of my difficult, terrible questions, and sorry I wrote so much.

>>>So did Paul, so you are in the best of company (1 Tim 1:5)! Go and love!

After this, I never heard back from N. I hope and pray that she came to a full understanding of the love and forgiveness of God.

I hope the same for everyone who reads this book. May you come to know how great is the Father's love for you. God loves you so much, and nothing can separate you from His love, not even the worst sin you have ever committed. God loves you!

About the Author

Jeremy Myers is an author, blogger, speaker, husband, and father. He is trying to follow Jesus into the world and in the process, has been led down some very strange paths. You can connect with Jeremy and learn more about his story through one of his blogs, or on one of the social networking sites below. Find his other books at RedeemingPress.com

Why You Have Not Committed the Unforgivable Sin was originally distributed as a free eBook to Jeremy's email newsletter subscribers. If you want to receive his future eBooks for free, subscribe today. He tries to send out 3-4 free eBooks per year.

Till He Comes – The main blog of Jeremy Myers where he writes to bring Scripture and Theology to Life.

Grace Commentary – A free, online Bible Commentary. This is a work in progress, and while there is not much on this site so far, more will be added in the near future.

Twitter – Follow Jeremy on Twitter @jeremyers1. He follows back!

Facebook – Like Jeremy on Facebook!

Google+ – Add Jeremy to one of your circles on Google. He will add you back.